# SEOUL
# SEOUL
# SEOUL

**NOTE TO THE READER**

1. The 50 places introduced in "*SEOUL SEOUL SEOUL*" were carefully selected based on the subjective perspectives of author Park Sunyoung and RAWPRESS Publishing House. These locations were chosen as the most authentic and inspiring places to experience Korean crafts in Seoul today.

2. When listing the 50 locations in the text, we followed the specific notation style used by each establishment category: gallery, shop, tea house, and dining. All other locations are noted in capital letters.

3. Terms related to Korean culture are written in italics.

4. For terms related to traditional Korean culture, explanatory endnotes have been provided. These are indicated with numbering in the main text and are further explained on the 'Glossary of Terms' page.

5. All endnotes are courtesy of author Park Sunyoung and RAWPRESS Publishing House.

6. Book titles appear in italics and within quotation marks, whereas exhibition titles are enclosed in quotation marks only.

# SEOUL
# SEOUL
# SEOUL

## A GUIDE TO SPACES OF CRAFT IN SEOUL

| | |
|---|---|
| PREFACE | 6 |
| GALLERY | 10 |
| SHOP | 52 |
| TEA HOUSE | 134 |
| DINING | 202 |
| GLOSSARY OF TERMS | 282 |

# A SLOW WAY TO EXPERIENCE THE MOST DYNAMIC VERSION OF SEOUL

PARK SUNYOUNG

Though it's late March, white snow falls. Yesterday was a warm spring day, making this sudden heavy snowfall a mix of bewilderment and delight. Watching the scene, I find today's weather strangely akin to Seoul itself: unpredictably shifting, a city where deeply rooted tradition and rapid trends coexist like two sides of a coin. It reveals unforeseen facets just when you think you understand it, a captivating entity that pushes its presence with urban complexity yet embraces you with its unique, nostalgic warmth. This multifaceted allure draws global attention to Seoul, at the far end of East Asia. Introducing myself as being from Seoul to someone in New York or Berlin often leads to an unending stream of questions about the city. In those moments, I sense a distant fascination behind their curiosity—a dreamlike image of a metropolis they have never seen. That is when I began to wonder about my own city, the place I have called home for 23 years.

    Having spent much of my life exploring European art and design, this curiosity felt like an opportunity: a chance to share Seoul's beauty with friends abroad, and to see my city through fresh eyes. It is only after viewing Seoul through the lens of others that I truly wanted to rediscover it myself. So I wandered its streets, letting my senses guide me. It became a journey of finding Seoul as a *Seoulite*. Surprisingly, I was drawn not to the fast-paced, flashy, or trendy spots, but to quieter corners: slow-paced neighborhoods, the warmth of tea carefully brewed, a dim museum alcove holding ancient ceramics, and thoughtful reinterpretations of traditional cuisine. Beneath Seoul's dynamic surface, I found a world of patience and care, where tradition and innovation coexist, and where skilled hands continually create something new. All of this led me to the word "craft." Not simply as beautiful objects or techniques, but as the act of shaping diverse materials and stories by hand. Furthermore, Korea has cultivated authentic daily life and aesthetic consciousness through craft since ancient times. Today, contemporary Korean artists continue this legacy with exceptional skill, sincerity, and thoughtful engagement with materials, enriching modern lifestyles with beauty and depth. Timeless objects—moon jars, patchwork *bojagi*, bamboo works, and celadon—continue to captivate collectors around the world.

    Metalwork artist Ryu Eunjung of the Studio FOH describes craft as "half heart, half object," and says she hopes to create things that feel like poetry. Poetic spaces, poetic objects, poetic people—these are what you will encounter in the fifty places featured in this book. Through them, you will discover the unique beauty, stories, and flavors shaped by Korean hands. Within these pages lies the authentic Seoul of today.

GAL

| | |
|---|---|
| 12 | SEOUL MUSEUM OF CRAFT ART |
| 18 | GALLERY WANNMUL |
| 22 | ARUMJIGI |
| 28 | GOBOKII |
| 32 | MOSOON |
| 38 | SPACE B-E |
| 42 | HANDLE WITH CARE |
| 48 | MONOHA HANNAM |

LERY

# SEOUL
# MUSEUM OF
# CRAFT ART

Craft has existed since the prehistoric era, ranging from the comb-pattern pottery of the Neolithic period and footed dishes, to fifth-century *Gaya* cups, seventh-century *Silla*[1] lidded containers with stamped patterns, *Goryeo*[2] bronze incense burners, silk wrapping cloths that once held precious ornaments, and wooden chests that stored *Joseon*[3] scholars' books. At the **Seoul Museum of Craft Art (SeMoCA)**, with its slogan "Craft for All, Museum for All," visitors can explore the long history of Korean craft—a tradition that possesses a beauty beyond mere utility and has been cherished by generations. Located at the entrance to Bukchon, it is an ideal stop on any Seoul itinerary and welcomes visitors of all ages.

    SeMoCA, nestled in the renovated buildings of Poongmoon Girls' High School, established in 1944, comprises seven buildings and a craft courtyard. The architectural charm lies in the low ceilings, numerous pillars, and intriguing passageways connecting

different wings, which preserve traces of its scholastic past. The striking sensory contrast—being immersed in the chrysanthemum pattern of a thousand-year-old *Ottchil*[4] chest, admiring mother-of-pearl or crane motifs carved into celadon-blue porcelain, and then gazing through the windows at contemporary Seoul unfolding before you—is a remarkable experience. After exploring Korea's craft history from antiquity to the present, visitors can move to the observatory on the fifth floor of the Children's Museum for a panoramic view of Bukaksan Mountain, Inwangsan Mountain, and the serene Anguk-dong landscape.

    SeMoCA's exhibitions encourage visitors to explore craft as a personal expression of taste and provide fresh inspiration. Examples include "Crafting the House" (2024), which reinterprets architectural elements through craft, and "The Palettes: Exploring Colors for Crafting" (2024). During these exhibitions, visitors can witness the infinite possibilities of craft—seeing 3D-printed roof tiles and furniture, multicolored windows made of glass and *Ottchil*, and *sobans*[5] crafted from PLA (a type of biodegradable plastic)—offering a glimpse into a vast horizon of craftsmanship. In short, SeMoCA represents an "ancient future," shaped by generations of diligent and thoughtful lives.

GALLERY

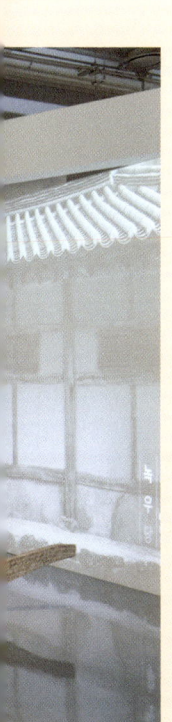

17

SEOUL MUSEUM OF
CRAFT ART
서울공예박물관

4, Yulgok-ro 3-gil, Jongno-gu, Seoul
@seoulmuseumofcraftart

# GALLERY WANNMUL

Since 2006, **gallery WANNMUL** has quietly chronicled the evolution of Korean craft, guided by an unwavering philosophy. Its name carries a dual meaning: objects to be playfully enjoyed and objects to be deeply appreciated. This essence mirrors the sentiment of Joseon-era scholars who planted countless varieties of azaleas in their courtyards, simply to savor their fleeting beauty.

    Just off the bustling streets of Cheongdam-dong, where global luxury brands dominate the landscape, gallery WANNMUL unfolds a timeless world of craftsmanship. Inside its two-story space, where lofty ceilings and expansive windows invite natural light, gold jewelry pieces gleam with quiet allure. The exhibition "Illuminating Gold" (焰金) (2024) showcases rings, brooches, and intricate pendants that explore gold's infinite expressive and decorative possibilities. The beautiful traces of engraving, carving, and refining reveal themselves only upon close

inspection. This exhibition transcends mere art jewelry display, offering a glimpse into gold's future potential for new scale and form. The exploration of materiality has been a key motif throughout the gallery's exhibitions. Notable shows include designer Choi Seulgi's furniture exhibition "Trace" (2022), featuring stainless steel frames combined with numerous leather papers, ceramist Yeo Byeonguk's "From" (2023), presenting his weighty ceramic world with drawing-like spatial dynamics, and metal craftsman Cho Sungho's "Layers of Time" (2024), where silver vessels cast from ancient rocks and trees through wax molds weave narratives of time and memory. gallery WANNMUL positions itself as an artistic companion, fostering deep relationships with artists who merge profound material understanding with creative expression. For those seeking to immerse themselves in contemporary Korean crafts, gallery WANNMUL offers an unparalleled encounter with artistry and tradition.

GALLERY WANNMUL
갤러리 완물

2F, 9, Samseong-ro 141-gil, Gangnam-gu, Seoul
@wannmul

# ARUMJIGI

Nestled beside *Gyeongbokgung*[6] Palace, the Arumjigi Foundation headquarters in Tongui-dong stand as one of Seoul's most compelling architectural achievements. Its exterior, a harmonious blend of concrete, glass, and wood that delineates each floor, eloquently expresses contemporary Korean sensibility and aesthetics.
A modest glass door set into the concrete facade serves as the main entrance, but when you ascend to the second floor, you are greeted by a spacious courtyard and a sizable *hanok*[7]. The decision to elevate the *hanok* and courtyard to the second floor, creating the effect of two distinct ground levels, is particularly striking. This unique and beautiful architectural design not only embodies the spirit of the foundation but also stands as an exhibition element in its own right. Moreover, opening the wooden sliding doors, which appear seamlessly integrated into the building's walls, reveals an elegant and majestic view of *Gyeongbokgung* Palace across the street. This is a perfect example of

"*chakyeong*"—a Korean architectural concept of "borrowing the view"—where the wide, rectangular frame encompassing the palace walls and tall trees creates an unforgettable, cinematic panorama of Seoul.

Since 2004, **Arumjigi** has curated exhibitions exploring traditional Korean culture through the themes of clothing, food, and shelter. These exhibitions encompass not only the *Joseon* Dynasty, but also the ancient lifestyles of the Three Kingdoms, *Goryeo*, and *Silla* periods, showcasing elements such as *hanbok*[8], ceremonial rites, tea culture, and even the floors and roof tiles of traditional architecture. Consequently, Arumjigi has uncovered the multi-layered aspects of Korea's cultural history while proposing contemporary interpretations. From this legacy, we discover remarkable crafts, including ceramics, *soban*, utensils, furniture, and textiles, which seamlessly integrate traditional elements into contemporary life. In the space titled "Softly Enclosed" from the exhibition "Room, As It Is" (2024), the pristine white *hanji*[9] walls, windows, and furniture demonstrate the modern versatility of traditional Korean paper. The casual placement of artwork and objects within the *hanok* space invites visitors to envision these elements as part of everyday life. Spending time at Arumjigi inspires a desire to live more beautifully and thoughtfully, using the wisdom and romanticism of past generations as a springboard for contemporary living.

GALLERY

ARUMJIGI  
아름지기

17, Hyoja-ro, Jongno-gu, Seoul  
@arumjigi

# GOBOKII

Atelier GOBOKII, tucked away on the second floor of Janghanpyeong's antique market, offers an intimate encounter with a private collection of vintage Korean furniture curated through personal narratives. Founded by Kim Jieun, the space embodies eight years of meticulous passion spent gathering Joseon-era *bandaji*[10], bookshelves, and cabinets, each piece resonates with the charm of objects that have weathered time. The name "GOBOKII" (古福囍) combines go (古), meaning "old," with bok (福) and hee (囍), forming an auspicious pattern representing longevity, fortune, and double happiness. It encapsulates the quiet delight of discovering happiness through things from the past. The space feels reminiscent of a cozy living room or study because her personal Le Corbusier LC2 chair, Charlotte Perriand's Méribel chair, and Pierre Chapo's round table harmonize in subtle tones with the understated wooden furniture from nineteenth-century Joseon. Visual delight comes from the layering of

pointed triangular patterns in the *geochimun* (geometric door design) meant to ward off evil spirits, blue sliding doors, and a circular red wall.

Each piece tells a hidden story: a wide, grounded cabinet from Gangwon-do, a two-tiered chest from Pyongyang with ornate cast-iron fittings and vibrant pigments, a bookshelf with *Yeouidumun* pattern (ruyi cloud motifs), its square proportions and dark tones evoking modern minimalism, and a portable medicine cabinet filled with tiny compartments. These century-old artifacts, with no known maker or household of origin, are brought to life through Kim's warm storytelling—inviting you into a distant, imagined era. On a spacious altar table once used for ancestral ceremonies, black ramie fabric is laid. Upon it, brass bowls, lidded containers, brass utensils, and a single camellia flower are arranged, creating a contemporary tableau of antiques. Atelier GOBOKII welcomes guests by appointment only, fostering intimate encounters with those who seek out this space. Alternatively, their small shop in the nearby Dapsimni Antique Market, open only on Saturdays from 11 AM to 4 PM, can be visited without reservation.

GOBOKII  
고복희

#201, 100, Gomisul-ro, Dongdaemun-gu, Seoul  
@gobokii_kr

# MOSOON

In Seoul's ever-changing heart, it's rare to find a neighborhood like Jeong-dong, which has preserved the city's appearance from a century ago. As you stroll along the tranquil stone wall path of *Deoksugung* Palace *Daehanmun*[11], weathered brick buildings catch your eye. Among them, the striking brick structure of the Shin-A Memorial Hall has stood for over a century. On the second floor of this historic building, **MOSOON** showcases refined, architectural works of contemporary Korean craft. Visitors are fortunate to encounter enigmatic objects such as *buncheong* pottery by ceramists Park Sungwook and Jeong Hyunwoo, and artworks carved from maple wood by woodcraft artist Park Kyungyoon.

    Director Kim Yeubin, whose background includes roles as art director at Artment.dep and marketer for "*Magazine B*," opened MOSOON out of a genuine love for craft. The space's layout, a series of small interconnected rooms, cleverly preserves the

building's original century-old structure, transforming the gallery into something akin to an indoor promenade. As you follow the fluid layout, the eclectic collection is displayed alongside furniture from various periods and origins—such as *Joseon* Dynasty *nong*[12], vintage Danish shelves, and British antique tables—making the pieces feel both familiar and sophisticated. Through monthly rotating exhibitions, MOSOON presents works by artists devoted to traditional techniques and personal expression, while also revealing the stories behind them. The director is a dedicated listener, meticulously documenting artists' personal narratives and philosophies alongside their techniques, which she often shares with visitors, offering insights into the artist, their work, and Korean craft.

During a visit to the "Night & Day" exhibition, I found Park Sungwook's works—his series of *buncheong* fragments stacked within an antique drawer—mysteriously evocative of secrets yet to be revealed. Within the walls of MOSOON, and along the journey there, one can truly experience the essence of Seoul's classical charm.

MOSOON
모순

#203, 33, Jeongdong-gil, Jung-gu, Seoul
@gallery_mosoon

# SPACE
# B-E

YOUNHYUN, known primarily as a specialized distributor of imported tiles, has transcended its original brand identity to become a significant influencer in Korea's cultural landscape. The company's slogan, "It's all about materials," encapsulates its fascinating approach, implemented in the YOUNHYUN Material Library—a playground of inspiration for enthusiasts of architecture and design, filled with wood, stone, glass, concrete, and fabric materials. This represents a sincere and ambitious commitment to exploring materiality, inspiring architecture and art beyond mere commercial interests.

While the showroom, which extends from the basement level to the second floor of the headquarters, showcasing rare and beautiful tiles, the third and fourth floors—named **SPACE B-E**—offer unexpected artistic landscapes. Through SPACE B-E by Younhyun has curated exhibitions such as "Paper is" (2020), "Soft Shelter" (2022), and "Dancing Grid" (2023), exploring

GALLERY

new possibilities of materials like paper, fabric, and tile as gentle assistants in life. This exploration in materiality naturally extends to craftsmanship, leading to collaborations with numerous Korean artisans and broadening the material spectrum. In the exhibition "Ambiguous Parang" (2024), illustrates this approach, where the subtle yet dignified jade hues of Cho Janghyun's celadon harmonize with the delicate blue tones imbued in the paper-thin white porcelain, creating a poetic and serene landscape that blends traditional craftsmanship with contemporary art.

    Walking through exhibition spaces that resemble new architectural forms created from woven fabrics and bamboo baskets, visitors are prompted to reflect. In this age of the immateriality, the act of drinking tea from a ceramist's cup or falling asleep on a hand-stitched pillow is surely an act of appreciating everyday life.

SPACE B-E
스페이스 비이

3F, Younhyun Bldg. 14, Hakdong-ro 26-gil,
Gangnam-gu, Seoul
@spacebe_official

# HANDLE WITH CARE

**Handle with Care** is a craft exhibition platform operated by the lifestyle brand TWL (Things We Love). Perched quietly on the top floor of the white, *hanji*-like TWL building on the hills of Noksapyeong, it offers a serene retreat. The building's most intriguing feature is its division into themes of time: seasons, permanence, daily life, and present moment across its floors.

    The experience begins on the first floor, where seasonal gifts are curated, followed by the second floor, showcasing timeless handcrafted pieces. The third floor is a haven of kitchenware and artisanal foods, leading to the fourth floor, home to Handle with Care, where the theme "Now: Exhibition" unfolds. Visitors arriving at this final destination are greeted with a warm welcome tea, a small yet thoughtful gesture.

    Handle with Care hosts exhibitions every three weeks, showcasing contemporary crafts that are both creative and authentic. Highlights include Sosayo's black porcelain resembling sculptures, and Lee

Soobin's mystical wooden animal objects crafted from various woods. It also includes Huh Sangwook's bold *buncheong* ceramics, and Kim Aram's poetic lacquer plates inspired by lunar and rocky surfaces. These exhibitions weave a narrative filled with tranquil, contemplative, and occasionally profound beauty.

Outside the window, Namsan Mountain rises majestically, reminding visitors that they are in the heart of Seoul. Inside, the eyes are drawn to the black, neatly arranged tools. These are the works of wood craftsman Jeong Donghoon, who works under the name Studio DEETE. He adds delicate lacquer to the wood, creating tools that make the tea ceremony even more special. From the tea tool box and tray to the tea cup shelf and tea table, the pieces exude the artist's dedication to creating objects that elevate the act of enjoying tea and are cherished even when not in use. Perhaps good objects are those that encourage us to live well. Like its name, Handle with Care aims to offer objects that will be treasured, age gracefully with their owners, and remain by their side for a long time. Appreciating each of these objects in the heart of Seoul is perhaps the most contemporary way to experience "Life in Seoul" today.

HANDLE WITH CARE
핸들위드케어

4F, 34, Noksapyeong-daero 40na-gil,
Yongsan-gu, Seoul
@twl_handlewithcare

# MONOHA
# HANNAM

Whenever heading to **MONOHA Hannam** in Hannam-dong, I always compelled to pause across the street and appreciate the building. The striking white, box-like concrete structure evokes a sense of anticipation with its absolute simplicity. Opened in 2020 in a renovated knitwear factory that operated for 50 years, MONOHA Hannam introduces the modern beauty of Korea, encompassing crafts, art, clothing that feels like a part of everyday life, and tableware.

  Turning into the narrow path behind the building, visitors encounter MONOHA Hannam's secret garden. The lush green of the moss covering the ground, the stone floor, and the autumn harmony of the *Cornus kousa, Stewartia pseudocamellia,* and *sapium japonicum* trees create a mystical path for visitors. Entering the vast white interior space, minimalist wooden furniture lines and ceramic curves emanate sculptural energy amid tranquility. Most striking is the forceful harmony of nine white porcelain pieces

displayed on nine pedestals. This scene is part of ceramist Kim Insik's exhibition "Flowing Time, Lingering Memories." The mysterious, destined patterns created by the *yeonrimun* technique[13]—layering and refining different white clay bodies—undulate like traditional landscape paintings. The meaning of crafts that MONOHA Hannam pursues is the genuine materiality and attitude towards life that contains the power of time, people, and fire. Here, everything creates its own context. The framed view through the large windows, a George Nakashima bench, the diagonal lines of the staircase railing, and a single dot in a Lee Ufan painting—all elements that reveal the interplay of space, objects, and the void in between. MONOHA Hannam allows visitors to sense the empty space flowing between artwork, space, and viewer—much like the 1960s Mono-ha art movement that emphasized the raw perception of space and objects through untouched earth, stone, wood, and paper.

MONOHA HANNAM  
모노하 한남

36, Dokseodang-ro, Yongsan-gu, Seoul  
@monoha_craft

S          H

| | |
|---|---|
| 54 | AREAPLUS |
| 60 | JANGSAENGHO |
| 64 | CHAPTER1 EDIT |
| 70 | WOL HANNAM |
| 74 | OBJECTIFY |
| 80 | ILSANGYEOBACK |
| 84 | NR CERAMICS |
| 90 | SOILBAKER |
| 94 | HOHODANG |
| 100 | HORANG |
| 104 | KYUBANGDOGAM |
| 110 | OJACRAFT |
| 114 | SIKIJANG |
| 120 | NARRATIVE OBJECT |
| 124 | TABLE OF CRAFT |
| 130 | LOFA SEOUL |

O P

# AREAPLUS

Stepping into the **AREAPLUS** showroom in the alleyways of Apgujeong-dong dissolves all preconceptions. The space, imbued with hushed stillness and subdued light, feels like stepping into a Giorgio Morandi still life, entirely removed from the outside world. Inside, objects, tableware, and small furniture designed by the interior and lifestyle studio Areaplus harmonize effortlessly with curated artisanal pieces.

More than a mere shop, this is a creative space shaped by Areaplus's refined sensibilities—honed through high-profile projects like the interiors for three-Michelin-starred Mingles, two-Michelin-starred Restaurant Allen, and one-Michelin-starred SOSEOUL Hannam, where custom furnishings were crafted to perfectly suit each environment. Like a corner of an impeccably curated lounge or kitchen, plates, candlesticks, cups, mirrors, and side tables are arranged with intentional precision throughout the

space. Their meticulous attention to detail extends to every element—from shelving and storage units to lighting fixtures and even the handles on doors and handrails. Areaplus's aesthetic flows with a quiet complexity that resists simple categorization. Traditional elements like *hanji* cabinet doors and intricately glazed bowls sit seamlessly alongside Western forms, such as softly hued goblets, cake stands, and delicate butter dishes.

    Founder Yu Ilsun, who spent his childhood overseas, brings an effortless sophistication to merging Western tableware aesthetics with Korean craftsmanship, reimagining both for modern living. Their *Yutnori*[1] set exemplifies this fusion—featuring four ebony pieces and circular brass game tokens inlaid with crystal, commanding admiration from any viewer. For those who seek rare, joyful objects—even if only to admire and not to own—and the stories that encapsulate them, few destinations are as fitting as the Areaplus showroom.

AREAPLUS  
에리어플러스

6-7, Eonju-ro 168-gil, Gangnam-gu, Seoul  
@areaplus

# JANG SAENGHO

Insa-dong is a neighborhood where traditional Korean culture thrives vibrantly. At Seoul's heart, its main street and alleys overflow with antique shops, traditional craft stores, galleries, and teahouses. Tucked away in one of these side streets lies a small, charming shop called **Jangsaengho**. It faces the serene tiled roof and stone walls of the *Min Byeongok House*[2]—a hanok built in the 1930s by renowned Korean architect Park Gilryong. Inside, this intimate space showcases contemporary tableware, vases, and tea utensils.

The first impression of Jangsaengho might be captured in two words: "tranquil and quiet." This aesthetic stems from owner Jung Hyonju's preference for serene and sophisticated items rather than bold or assertive objects. A Joseon-era *Hwajodo*[3] featuring a pair of birds adorns the wall, while a single crimson winter camellia rests in a delicate glass vase crafted by ceramist Kim Dongwan. Elegant plates, bowls, and teacups from Haeinyo gather in harmony, like a well-balanced family, while Hong Doohyeon's flowing teapots and luminous white porcelain pieces bring clarity to both eye and spirit. Here, modest objects gather to create an exquisite harmony. The name Jangsaengho—meaning "a jar painted with lasting vitality"—was bestowed years ago by poet Kim Sangok

upon her parents' antique shop at the entrance of Insa-dong. While studying ceramics, Jung Hyonju found herself drawn to the world of craft, leading her to open Jangsaengho in 2017. This venture marked her distinct path in contemporary craftsmanship, diverging from her parents' antique trade. She envisions the shop as a welcoming *sarangbang*[4]—a traditional Korean reception room—where artists and visitors can gather to share stories. As I stepped outside, the season's first snow had begun to fall over Insa-dong, transforming its streets and sky into a pristine white canvas—a fitting finale to a visit to this haven of contemporary craft.

JANGSAENGHO  
장생호

23-4, Insadong 10-gil, Jongno-gu, Seoul  
@jangsaengho

# CHAPTER 1
# EDIT

The building housing **Chapter1 EDIT**, formerly the Sinsajang Inn, lacks large display windows, making it difficult to discern its nature from the outside. The narrow entrance stairway creates an even greater sense of anticipation. Inside the Indian pink-hued space on the second floor, numerous craft pieces harmoniously blend with 20th-century masterpiece furniture by Pierre Jeanneret and Oscar Niemeyer, creating an unfamiliar yet captivating beauty.

    Founded in 2018 as an extension of Chapter1, a lifestyle select store dedicated to Korean contemporary craftsmanship, Chapter1 EDIT was conceived to explore the artistry of handmade furniture, objects, and the unique sensibility of craft. From the second to fourth floors, the collection flows like a long symphony across distinctly conceptualized spaces, featuring everything from tableware and decorative pieces to cutlery, *soban*, sofas, and tables. Beyond rough concrete pillars, the ceiling is adorned

with a lamp by metal artist Kim Gyeok, woven from thin metal like a net. On the third floor, shelves lining one wall display an array of vessels, including ceramist Kim Gyosik's innocent and whimsical ceramic dinosaurs and Yoon Taesung's ethereal glass vases. The shelving unit, inspired by old Southeast Asian apothecary cabinets, seems to offer comfort and joy through its contents.

Practical trays, plates, glasses, and coasters are thoughtfully arranged on a low-set table, while the walls feature Slowdown Studio's vibrant, patterned blankets. Despite their diverse origins, these pieces blend together with remarkable harmony-a testament to the space's excellence in layering individual pieces

SHOP

to create unique aesthetics and landscapes.

The fourth floor takes a subtle approach, incorporating craft pieces among larger furniture elements. Here, Still Life brand's mint-colored sofa, developed by Chapter1, Kar Studio's clay-like chairs and tables, and woodcraft artist Park Honggu's black *soban* harmonize in darkness and tranquility. The space offers a surprising experience where multiple layers of beauty converge into a single, powerful impression.

CHAPTER1 EDIT
챕터원 에디트

65, Naruteo-ro, Seocho-gu, Seoul
@chapter1_edit

# WOL HANNAM

The octagonal tea tray by metal craftsman Kim Donggyu and the luminous glass cup by glass artist Kim Donghee are treasured pieces in my kitchen collection that I use frequently. By "treasured," I mean that I both cherish them deeply and use them often at my dining table. I purchased these items from **WOL Hannam**, a place where beautiful yet functional craft objects consistently captivate me. Within the space, each piece asserts its own presence: metal artist Park Mikyung's lacquered placemats where blue manifests like the sky, ceramist Lee Kijo's footed bowls reminiscent of smooth white Joseon-era porcelain, and ceramist Kim Kyutae's objects resembling fruits from faded still-life paintings. CEO Cho Sunglim, whose desire to share food and tea with friends is the driving force behind this exquisite curation, has long explored exceptional tableware and utensils.

    The name "WOL" is an acronym formed from the first letters of "Work," "Object," and "Life." The

SHOP

shop was founded with the hope that, born from the quiet dedication of creators (work), works (objects) would naturally become part of customers' daily lives (life). Unlike WOL Samcheong, which presents exhibitions in an open *hanok* setting, WOL Hannam offers an intimate, private ambiance, as if customers were glimpsing into someone's cherished kitchen

cabinet. Entering WOL Hannam on the second floor of the building that also houses the teahouse Chachaithé, customers are greeted by sunlight streaming through the shadows of green leaves that reach into the space. The glass cups on a lacquered *hanji* table then catch the light and sparkle. The objects displayed on the monochrome metal bookshelves create a harmonious and symbolic arrangement, like precious antiques in a *chaekgado*[5]. Choosing just one item from among many becomes a journey of self-discovery. Crafts, after all, imbue our lives with tangible character as they coexist with us, marking life's moments—from inviting someone over for a meal to arranging seasonal flowers. Moreover, there is something enchanting about the finite nature of craft, which wears down and sometimes even breaks according to the user's habits!

WOL HANNAM  
월 한남

3F, 74, Itaewon-ro 54-gil, Yongsan-gu, Seoul  
@wol.co.kr

# OBJECTIFY

At the heart of craftsmanship lies a quiet act of care. A thoughtful white porcelain bowl that keeps food warm a little longer, the smooth grain of a wooden knife handle, and the delicate curve of a teacup's rim that kisses the lips—these mindful gestures make objects not only functional but lasting companions in our daily lives. Located in Yeonhui-dong, **objectify** introduces curated artisanal objects that enrich our everyday lives. The selection spans Korean contemporary crafts, *Joseon*-era antique furniture, Japanese vintage pieces, and a subtle aroma layered with various incenses, smudging sticks, and candles that tranquilly unite to permeate the space. Movable partitions that enable functional transformations of the space, wall shelves filling the front like a library, and light filtering through *hanji*-finished large windows hint at the intriguing activities and atmosphere unfolding within.

Highlights include Dito 140's plates etched

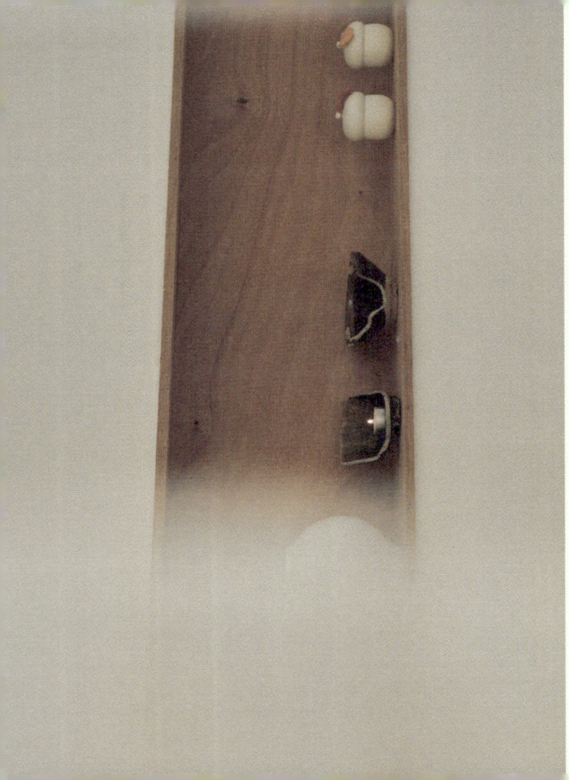

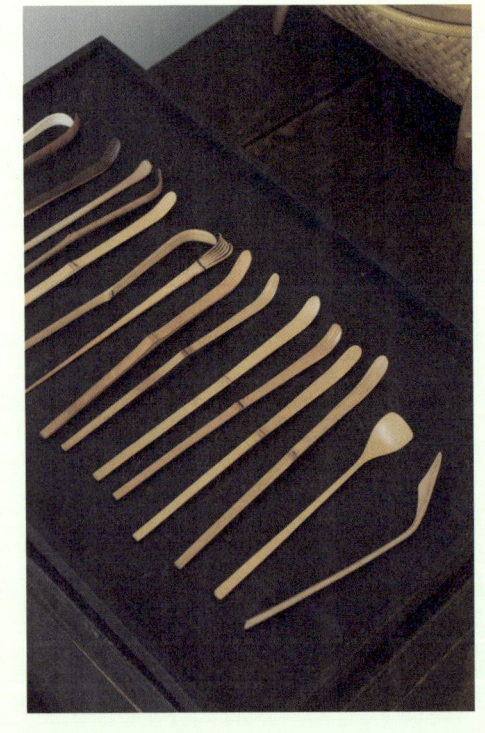

with the textured weave of ramie fabric, ceramist Kim Doheon's round plates where the flow of glaze expresses cosmic minerals, ceramist Kyung Sihyun's dessert pedestal plates adorned with rich texture through silver applied over ceramic, and woodcraft artist So Neungseon's butter knife carving the fluid movement of killifish from cherry wood. The selection by CEOs Han Seungchul and Park Jiye encompasses objects of deep and pure craft contemplation, quality materials, and meticulous labor—befitting objectify's ethos of redefining things. Even fragmented ceramics and dried flowers find renewed purpose here, arranged as poetic vignettes. Photography is not permitted—a gesture encouraging you to engage deeply with each piece through touch and contemplation rather than through a lens. objectify's insistence on tactile discovery invites you to refine their own sensibilities, one carefully crafted object at a time.

OBJECTIFY
오브젝티파이

2F, 3-4, Yeonhuimat-ro, Seodaemun-gu, Seoul
@objectify_official

# ILSANG
# YEOBACK

Discovering an exquisite shop while leisurely strolling through a neighborhood can feel like an unexpected gift, bringing an even greater sense of joy. Nestled in a quiet alley of Seochon, **ilsangyeoback** is a craft shop that encompasses everything from functional tableware to *objets d'art*, as well as antiques like old *soban* and *chanhap* (traditional Korean food boxes). A diverse selection awaits, where traditional Korean antiques meet modern Korean craftmanship. Among them, pure white ceramics and vessels, elegantly displayed behind large windows, stop passersby in their tracks.

      Han Shinyoung, the owner who has worked as a ceramist, envisioned becoming an exceptional mediator between artisans and artists who create vessels and the customers who use them. Her curated selection at Ilsangyeoback features a wide range of beautifully crafted pieces that excel in functionality, form, and durability. The "back" in ilsangyeoback doesn't refer to the color white, but rather the number one hundred (百), reflecting the shop's philosophy of curating more than just 100 meaningful items for long-term use.

Ilsangyeoback showcases an impressive array of works: ceramist Yoon Sanghyun's vessels layered with mysterious blue glaze, Yoo Yeonju's plates with textures reminiscent of hemp fabric, glass artist Lee Kihoon's candy-like bowls formed by laying thin glass threads

over blown shapes, and ceramist Kim Panki's enormous *dalhangari*[6], so massive it cannot be embraced even with both arms. The shop's main structure, functioning like a *hanok*'s wooden floor, creates a rhythmic arrangement of displayed items. Moreover, the pure white *hanji* walls and ceiling-draped white fabrics provide a perfect backdrop for white porcelain pieces, which form the backbone of Korean ceramics. As one encounters each vessel at ilsangyeoback, a desire grows to fill them with home-cooked dishes. It seems that crafts could become the perfect companion for the wholesome, modest hours spent nurturing a home.

ILSANGYEOBACK
일상여백

12-15, Jahamun-ro 17-gil, Jongno-gu, Seoul
@ilsangyeoback

# N R
# CERAMICS

The **NR CERAMICS** showroom, newly relocated to Bukchon, occupies the second floor of a local supermarket on Gyedong-gil. Ascending the stairs, customers encounter a tidy, beige-toned space where the textures of dark wood, ceramics, and *hanji* paper intertwine, creating an atmosphere that subtly blends Korean aesthetics with Southern European charm. The space's identity becomes even more enigmatic with hemp fabric shades and an indistinct, soothing soundtrack, drawing visitors' attention to the textures of ceramics, the curves of objects, and the warm yellow light emanating from *hanji*.

      Established in 2018 by ceramist Lee Nuri, NR CERAMICS is a brand dedicated to crafting vessels that effortlessly blend into everyday life. From plates and bowls to cups and vases, the brand's aesthetic appeal lies in its gently twisted curves and asymmetrical details, which reveal different forms depending on the viewing angle. Observing the slightly

uneven edges of the plates, the concave surfaces of the vases, and the white, blue, and black pieces enriched with the depth of their glaze evokes a sense of longing. It is a desire to keep these pieces close, even without the need for flowers or food. Striking a balance between functionality and beauty, NR CERAMICS' creations convey a sensory pleasure and depth, serving as mediators that restore unique textures and narratives to our lives.

The showroom's gray-tiled floor, a Thonet rocking chair in the corner, and an African sculpture resting atop a *Joseon*-era *bandaji* chest create a quiet tension, where objects from different times and places coexist. Founder Lee Nuri draws inspiration from the natural beauty and simple yet powerful crafts of Portugal, where she currently resides. Leveraging this influence, the showroom has enriched its ambiance by featuring jewelry from the Portuguese brand SONSONOR and works by Portuguese artisans, adding further depth to its experience.

NR CERAMICS
엔알세라믹스

2F, 99, Gyedong-gil, Jongno-gu, Seoul
@nrceramicsofficial

# SOIL
# BAKER

Jeongdong-gil is an area where seasonal changes are particularly pronounced, its vitality enhanced by the harmony between tall street trees and aged red brick buildings. Nestled on the second floor of the elegant Shin-A Memorial Hall is the **SOILBAKER** showroom. Inside the airy, off-white space, bold tables and shelves are lined with an extensive selection of ceramic pieces. Through the windows, the view of *Jungmyeongjeon* Hall—once King Gojong's office building—offers a momentary escape from the present. SOILBAKER, meaning "one who bakes soil," is a tableware brand that explores the possibilities of ceramics through the collaborative efforts of ceramists, designers, and chefs.

    Launched in 2015 by Yang Hyerin, who studied industrial design and culinary arts in New York, the brand emerged from her experiences working in restaurants, with a vision to create tableware that is both aesthetically refined and highly functional. SOILBAKER's greatest appeal lies in its diverse collection, which features not only everyday tableware for the home but also pieces crafted to elevate the presentation of dishes in restaurants. The "Sando Set for One," designed for individuals living alone, includes five pieces such as a plate, a rice bowl, and a soup bowl. For newlyweds setting up their new home, there are the "Set for Two" and "Set for Four." Their collection also features tea sets, earthenware pots, various sized plates, and cutlery. "Crumbs," with its raw clay texture,

"Sando," offering subtle elegance with its soft glaze, and "Dots," reminiscent of scattered paint splatters—these are SOILBAKER's beloved signature collections. Each piece radiates a distinct beauty, shaped by the natural variations in clay and glaze. The tableware is displayed on tables made from different materials, including wood and marble. On one side, a sink setup invites customers to envision these pieces in their own homes while they browse. The true pleasure of SOILBAKER vessels lies in their satisfying tactile quality, offering a sensory experience that bridges traditional craftsmanship with contemporary design.

SOILBAKER
소일베이커

#202, 33, Jeongdong-gil, Jung-gu, Seoul
@soilbaker

# HOHODANG

Since ancient times, Koreans have beautifully commemorated both life's milestones and the changing of seasons. From celebrating a child's first birthday to beginning formal education and marriage, people exchanged meaningful gifts laden with wishes and congratulations. With the arrival of *Dano*[7], the festival welcoming early summer, it was customary to gift fans to ward off the heat, while on *Dongji*[8], people shared bowls of red bean porridge, believed to drive away misfortune. These traditions reflect the warmth and sentiment embedded in Korean life.

Nestled in Cheongdam-dong, **HOHODANG** embodies this spirit with its philosophy: "May only good things come your way." Founder Yang Jungeun opened Hohodang in 2010, inspired by her fondest childhood memories of sharing holiday meals prepared by her mother. For fifteen years, she has meticulously crafted items that maintain traditional techniques while coming along with contemporary life—*hanbok*,

*bojagi*, traditional medicine pouches, and traditional tea trays.

    Bathed in soft sunlight and overlooking a lush garden, Hohodang is filled with items that hold deep stories and heartfelt wishes. A pair of lacquered wooden wild geese, a symbolic wedding gift for a harmonious marriage, delicately embroidered *baenaet-jeogori*[9] adorned with zodiac animals and deer, a pure white silk hanbok for a baby's hundredth day celebration, *Ipchuncheop*[10], handwritten calligraphy scrolls once affixed to doors and pillars to welcome prosperity in the new year, and handcrafted brass spoons and chopsticks neatly tucked in quilted pouches—each item carries a sense of tradition and

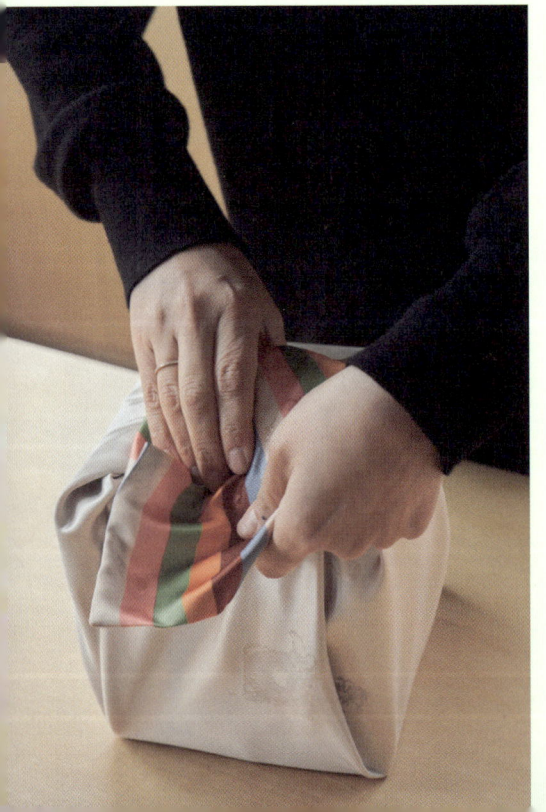

affection. Regardless of any gift, Hohodang's true artistry lies in its thoughtful wrapping. Every item is carefully packaged in vibrant *bojagi*[11], *yangdan*[12], ramie, or *nobang*[13], and secured with a delicate *Dongshimgyeol*[14] knot, a symbol of enduring bonds and heartfelt blessings. More than just a wrapping—it is a gesture of wishing each recipient a life filled with good fortune and happiness.

HOHODANG
호호당

2F, 17, Apgujeong-ro 72-gil, Gangnam-gu, Seoul
@hohodang_official

# HORANG

**Horang** presents cutlery and knives that reflect the refined sensibilities of Korean craft, guided by the motto "Sculptures for Everyday Life." The brand's philosophy centers on creating enduring pieces meant to be treasured and used daily, a vision brought to life through the mastery of local artisans. In Korea, the spoon and chopsticks set—known as *sujeo*—has been an essential part of daily rituals since the *Goryeo* Dynasty, symbolizing not only culinary tradition but also the broader cultural identity of the Korean people.

Aiming to carry forward the legacy of Korean *sujeo*—the only metal utensil tradition in East Asia—Horang's flatware is crafted from premium stainless steel, offered in a variety of finishes such as silver, gold, matte, and black. Each piece features graceful, hand-shaped curves and meticulous detailing, with a personalized engraving service that transforms everyday objects into meaningful works of art.

The brand's cozy showroom in Seochon, Seoul,

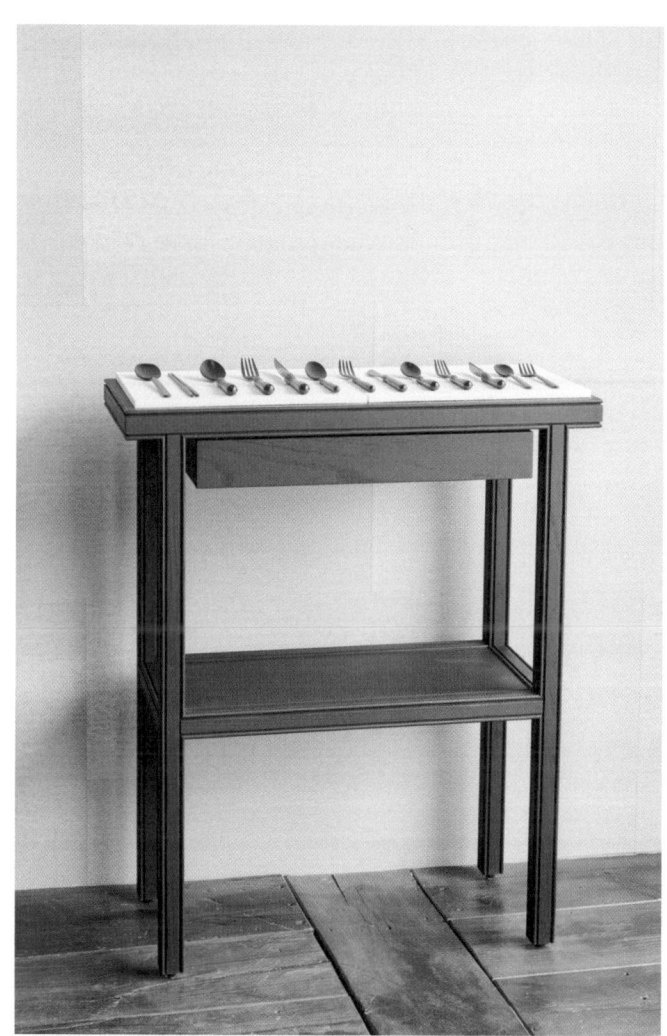

spans just ten *pyeong*, approximately 33 square meters, and showcases five unique cutlery styles—spoon, regular, table, dessert, and mini—displayed like polished jewelry. The space itself is a restored *hanok*, originally constructed in 1965 and revived by master craftsman Kwon Hyukyul using traditional methods like yellow clay plaster and exposed wooden rafters. Traces of old newspaper on reclaimed pillars and the deep, ink-stained wooden floors reveal a layered,

handcrafted character throughout the interior. Artisan collaborations further enrich the atmosphere: a brass handle by metalworker Kim Jaeyoon, a charred-wood counter by wood artisan Park Honggu, and delicate *hanji* window screens handmade by master paper artist Lee Jasung from Cheongsong. Light gently filters through these paper doors, filling the space with a soft glow. A wall finished in subtle gray is adorned with a custom washi paper mural from Kamisoe Kyoto, its surface textured with crushed shells, providing a tranquil backdrop for the minimalist cutlery displays. At the counter, an Isamu Noguchi "Akari No. 9" lamp sits as a reminder of the belief of the founder, Bae Yonghee,—echoing Noguchi—that "art should become a part of everyday life for everyone." At Horang, that vision is realized, even a spoon becomes a vessel of heritage, design, and human connection.

HORANG
호랑

40, Jahamun-ro, Jongno-gu, Seoul
@the_horang

# KYUBANG DOGAM

Tucked away in a quiet alley of Anguk-dong, a modest hanok draws the eye with a name inscribed on its wall: Kyubangdogam-jip. Translating roughly to "House of the Women's Quarter Culture," the name signals a mission to honor and reinterpret the domestic artistry once cultivated in Korea's traditional inner quarters. **Kyubangdogam** is a heritage textile brand that reintroduces hand-sewn household items—such as bedding, baby garments, and aprons—infused with cultural memory and refined craftsmanship. Established in 2006 by handcraft artist Woo Youngmi, the brand breathes life into natural fibers like *mumyeong*[15], silk, and ramie—materials deeply embedded in Korea's everyday past. With careful stitching and embroidery, these understated textiles are transformed into works that embody the serene grace of Korean aesthetics. From bedcovers inspired by the opulent phoenix motifs of the *Goryeo* Dynasty to airy summer blankets made of *chunpo*[16]—a breezy fabric

once favored in warm seasons—Kyubangdogam's pieces remain rooted in heritage while thoughtfully adapted for contemporary living. The brand also offers bespoke creations that capture personal stories, wishes, and sentiments, woven directly into the designs. This deeply personal approach reflects the brand's dedication to sincere, human-centered craft—and continues under the direction of Lee Geonwoo, who brings a fresh perspective to the legacy founded by Woo.

Some works carry symbolic blessings for newborns, drawing from *taemong* (conception dreams) or Chinese zodiac signs based on the child's birth year. These are expressed through lovingly reimagined motifs—from the *sipjangsaeng* to the *sagunja*[17]. A yellow baby blanket, for instance, features a rabbit playfully weaving through bookcases, while a plain cotton swaddle depicts a coiled snake among butterflies, clouds, and plantain leaves. These heirloom-quality items, while designed for sleep, often become treasured keepsakes or wall hangings—objects imbued with affection and intention. Within the space, a rich tapestry of materials—luminous silks and unbleached cotton—fills reconstructed Joseon-era wardrobes and storage chests, while cushions and pillows are layered throughout, inviting visitors to sit, listen, and linger. Time seems to soften as guests hear the story behind each piece. Housed in a carefully restored L-shaped *hanok* dating back over a century, the Kyubangdogam showroom occupies a compact room near the main gate—serving as a contemporary reimagining of the women's quarters. Across the courtyard lies a dining area, where customers can enjoy seasonally curated Korean meals. These refined set menus—such as tender sliced pork, braised short ribs, or golden tilefish—are thoughtfully prepared by Woo herself, whose skill at the table matches her artistry with thread and fabric.

KYUBANGDOGAM  
규방도감

24-4, Bukchon-ro 1-gil, Jongno-gu, Seoul  
@kyubangdogam

# OJACRAFT

The **Ojacraft** showroom, nestled on the third floor of a small building in Yeonhui-dong, feels like stepping into a single piece of pottery, expanded into a space for artistic expression. Artist Oja, who majored in ceramics before spending over two decades as a graphic designer, found that returning to pottery in his mid-30s became a holistic healing experience for his weary body and soul.

    The showroom, a harmonious blend of Oja's diverse creations and carefully curated negative space, welcomes visitors with a whimsical yet modest atmosphere. Its distinct character is enriched by painterly photographs taken by his artistic collaborator, Jebi. Together, they crafted shelves and tables from salvaged wood and deliberately scattered fragments of broken pottery across the floor.

    Ojacraft's signature pieces, consistently cherished by collectors, include elongated oval and octagonal plates with vintage-inspired gray and timeworn black finishes, along with incense holders shaped like swallows, finger foxes, and rocking horses. These objects, reminiscent of childhood comfort toys, carry meaning beyond their function. The quiet power of these creations is evident in pieces like the Demian Vase, which, when inverted, transforms from a baby's head into a flower vase, or becomes a candleholder when upright. Upon entering the showroom, visitors

can choose between the bright room on the left and the dark room on the right. The bright space displays tableware such as plates, bowls, and cups, while the dark space features vases bearing cracks from the kiln, a large plate seemingly stitched together with thread, and a lamp with a white ceramic shade. Just as Oja considers himself an artist rather than a ceramist, this space evokes unpredictable scenes and sensations.

OJACRAFT
오자크래프트

3F, 24, Yeonhui-ro 11ga-gil, Seodaemun-gu, Seoul
@ojacraft

# SIKIJANG

**SIKIJANG** is both a beautiful tableware shop and a world that unfolds the diverse spectrum of craft. Since its opening in 2005, it has maintained its distinctiveness by consistently showcasing works by Korean artisans whose craftsmanship transcends trends. The name "Sikijang" carries dual meaning: it refers both to master craftsmen who create vessels and to traditional storage cabinet for precious kitchenware.

Founder Chung Soyeong, a long-time craft enthusiast, acts more as a producer who brings forth artisans' imagination, spirit, and exceptional techniques in presenting their works. This is what sets SIKIJANG apart from other curated shops, allowing visitors to savor the joy of life through the simple act of choosing a piece of kitchenware. The spacious ground floor resembles a library, with tall shelves brimming with cups, plates, teapots, bowls, and cutlery. Here, you'll find metal artist Jung Yuri's lacquered placemats, glass artist Kim Jeongeun's ethereal cups

with tweed patterns created from delicate glass threads, metal artist Lim Mungul's wine cooler made of thinly hammered copper with lacquer finish, and glass artist Kim Kira's plates incorporating precious Kanazawa silver leaf between glass layers.

As I handled the particularly enchanting pieces among the many, I could feel the vivid touch and breath of their creators—the joy of creation felt in unity with the works, encompassing techniques learned through experience and the excellence of materials. Ascending to the upper floor, a solid space unfolds, resembling a comfortable living room or a corner of a dining room by a window. There, you can experience the joy of encountering layers of furniture, tableware, and objects created by craft artists within the scale and illumination of daily life. At that moment, afternoon sunlight streamed through the low shelves filled with *sobans*, the generously sized bowls with checkered patterns on white porcelain, and the brass-colored lighting and hangers. My gaze was drawn to sleek stools and tables casting shadows on the floor—furniture created by metal artist Choi Seulgi, who achieves unique forms and durability by layering leather paper thickly over metal. SIKIJANG is a place that captures the infinite expressions and energy shaped by clay, glass, and metal—and the boundless potential of craft itself.

SIKIJANG
식기장

1F, 9, Samseong-ro 141-gil, Gangnam-gu, Seoul
@sikijang_official

# NARRATIVE
# OBJECT

The name of Ttukseom, a popular recreational park at the entrance of Seongsu-dong, originates from the *dukgi* (纛旗), a flag erected to pray for victory when the army went on an expedition during the *Joseon* Dynasty. Kim Yewon, who shared this historical anecdote of Ttukseom—where a *dukgi* covered with red fur was hung and a ritual held for King Chiucheon (蚩尤天王), a legendary goblin—runs **NARRATIVE OBJECT** near Ttukseom. She co-owns the business with her husband, Kim Jaeyun, a former carpenter specializing in *hanok* construction. Longing for a hands-on lifestyle close to nature, the couple opened NARRATIVE OBJECT after living in Berlin and Cheongdo, Gyeongsangbuk-do, Korea, creating a shop that reflects their daily life aspirations.

    Despite its proximity to Seoul Forest, one of Seoul's trendiest spots, a quiet warmth enveloped me upon entering the shop. The wood-toned interior and all the furniture were handcrafted by Kim Jaeyun,

showcasing his carpentry expertise. In the sunlit space, porcelains imbued with a wild energy by ceramist Choi Jaehoon are displayed alongside elegant *buncheong* teacups adorned with peonies, butterflies, and insects painted with blue pigments by ceramist Kwon Kihyun. Additionally, a Pensive Bodhisattva statue by Lee Taeho, created using the *kkeomeok* smoking firing technique[18] emanates a mystical presence from its shelf.

NARRATIVE OBJECT's Instagram profile reads, "From Korean Heritage to Contemporary Folk Art." The couple prefers to call their shop a "folk art shop" (*minye shop*), emphasizing the simplicity and everyday connection of folk art over traditional crafts. They gravitate towards *minye*—more modest and intimate than traditional crafts—as it better reflects their sensibility and connection to daily life. This ethos is evident in their curated selection, which includes

organic clothing from brands like OAGE and Wardrobe.41, as well as ramie tea mats, antique brass spoons, lambskin room shoes, and woven baskets. Throughout my visit to NARRATIVE OBJECT, I was filled with a warm, rustic emotion, reminiscent of a faded sweater knitted by my grandmother.

NARRATIVE OBJECT  
내러티브 오브젝트

1F, 24-7, Seoulsup 2-gil, Seongdong-gu, Seoul  
@narrative.object

# TABLE OF CRAFT

**Table of Craft (TOC.)**, a lifestyle shop with the motto "Everyday Craft," offers an intriguing perspective on the integration of craft into everyday life. Rather than strictly adhering to traditional interpretations, Table of Craft's selection focuses on pieces that reflect contemporary tastes. Instead of heavy, somber craftwork, they favor items that can be casually incorporated into everyday routines. The shop features an array of delightful objects that can add a touch of joy to any room, particularly the kitchen: from bamboo tea baskets from Damyang to transparent glass vases by glass artist Kim Dongwan, Dojayeon's teacups with a rustic, handmade feel, and tiny *dalhangari* painted with round, smiling faces by ceramist Kim Jihyun.

Located on the fourth floor of the charming ARGO building in Apgujeong, Table of Craft distinguishes itself from other craft shops with its cheerful and vibrant atmosphere. This ambiance stems from a harmonious blend of elements: sunlight

flooding the pristine, bright white interior, a mint-colored handrail on the stairs, a long birchwood table draped with a pale green tablecloth, and striking furniture from Africa and India.

 A centerpiece lamp woven specifically for Table of Craft by textile artist Jung Eunsil serves as the space's focal point, radiating positive energy through its densely woven threads and the use of the five cardinal colors. Crafts have always served as authentic touchstones in simple daily acts, such as cooking rice and brewing tea. There is a distinct pleasure in carefully handling a single bowl or cup, as if it carries memories.

As the straightforward message written on Table of Craft's wall in brush calligraphy proclaims, "Craft is good." From a broom made of *Hansan mosi*[19] and a goblin-shaped candleholder carved in Wonju, Gangwon-do, to pottery crafted from clay in Melbourne, Australia—Table of Craft invites customers to linger and truly appreciate each object until they find something that resonates with them. When the pace slows amidst these beautiful things, it is the perfect opportunity to head upstairs and enjoy a relaxing cup of tea at Ado Gyeyoungbae.

TABLE OF CRAFT
테이블 오브 크래프트

4F, 16, Eonju-ro 173-gil, Gangnam-gu, Seoul
@table.of.craft

# L O F A
# S E O U L

**LOFA Seoul** is perhaps the lifestyle concept store that most closely resembles Seoul. Objects with blurred boundaries between art and design—trendy yet mysteriously unidentifiable in origin—emanate an enigmatic charm. This unique atmosphere is shaped by the inventive perspectives of the LOFA Seoul team members, who curate items that infuse their space with wit and vibrancy.

    The LOFA Seoul showroom in Sinyongsan draws inspiration from the "*mugaji*"—the free newspapers and magazines distributed at subway and bus stations in the mid-2000s. Much like the *mugaji*'s embrace of subculture and creative freedom, the store aims to discover compelling items and share the engaging stories behind intriguing brands and objects. Consequently, once inside the showroom, it is easy to lose track of time amidst the captivating array of over 2,000 items alongside various books, fashion pieces, and artworks. Among the highlights are earthy vases

and tableware by ceramist Lee Myungjin, and pastel-toned oval plates by PEON, whose imperfect forms bring a relaxed charm to the table.

At the back of the showroom, a vending machine named "Searchlight" glows softly. This machine dispenses kits containing mini art books—collections of process fragments and journals from twelve different artists—offering a playful chance to own a genuine piece of an artist's journey for just 8,000 won. It's this kind of unexpected delight that captures LOFA Seoul's distinctive appeal. Products like ceramic by ceramist Yoon Jihoon and cutlery by metalwork artist Oh Subin are the result of "Lo-factory," LOFA Seoul's own manufacturing initiative that merges each creator's identity with the store's production system. The forms and textures of these pieces, which seem poised to brighten a corner of daily life, invite exploration. As you wander among the bold designs and stacks of books, it becomes clear that LOFA Seoul is a playground for grown-ups—a place where rediscovering a sense of wonder is not only possible, but inevitable. Here, there's a moment when something on the shelf truly becomes your own.

LOFA SEOUL
로파 서울

3F, 21, Hangang-daero 11-gil, Yongsan-gu, Seoul
@lofa_seoul

T
H O

| | |
|---|---|
| 136 | SANSUHWA TEAHOUSE |
| 142 | DADORE TEAROOM |
| 146 | MONGJAE |
| 152 | CHACHA TEA CLUB BUKCHON LOUNGE |
| 156 | DELPHIC ANGUK FLAGSHIP STORE |
| 162 | ADO GYEYOUNGBAE |
| 166 | EEUM |
| 172 | 1994SEOUL |
| 176 | CHACHAITHÉ |
| 182 | MAGPIE&TIGER SINSA TEAROOM |
| 186 | OSULLOC TEA HOUSE BUKCHON |
| 192 | OMOT |
| 196 | TOVE |

# SANSUHWA TEAHOUSE

Going out for tea always adds a touch of splendor to life. The simple decision to enjoy a cup amid the daily hustle etches a gentle detail onto my existence. **Sansuhwa Teahouse**, nestled in a quiet alley of Hannam-dong, has remained a haven for 11 years since 2014. The first-floor tearoom, with its large windows, is ideal for a casual cup of tea and a selection of desserts. The second-floor *Dasil* (tearoom), accessible by reservation, hosts more formal tea gatherings and classes.

Jung Hyejoo, the founder, with her soft voice and elegant movements, presents me with "Bai Hao Yinzhen," a premium white tea—one of over 80 varieties on Sansuhwa Teahouse's extensive tea list. I watch the tea cascade into a cobalt-blue *Gongdobae*[1], a piece by her favored ceramist, Cho Janghyun. The cup's refined form, with its sharp brim, displays a touch of intriguing boldness in the artisan's exquisite finish. The unconventional design of the teaware—including a

cocktail glass-like *sukwoo*[2], lidless teapots, and uniquely shaped vessels—influences both our actions and perspectives, enriching the tea experience.

For Jung Hyejoo, who grew up immersed in tea culture under her tea-loving mother's influence, Sansuhwa Teahouse represents a world that harmoniously blends tea, space, and people. Her resilience over the past ten years, in a city dominated by coffee culture, has established Sansuhwa Teahouse as one of Seoul's most renowned teahouses. Beyond serving fine teas, she is now dedicated to showcasing talented although lesser-known artisans. Through her initiative, the PADO Institute for the Study for Historical Objects, she highlights tea culture artifacts, while the newly opened underground exhibition space, BAAT, marks a quiet beginning in fostering a contemporary appreciation for craft. Behind the bustling tea preparation bar, shelves lined with *Gaiwans*[3], *Gongdobaes*, glass fairness cups, and tea warmers resemble a museum display. To me, Sansuhwa Teahouse is more than a teahouse—it's a sanctuary, a true "tea paradise."

SANSUHWA TEAHOUSE  21-14, Hannam-daero 20-gil, Yongsan-gu, Seoul
산수화 티하우스  @sansuhwatea

# DADORE
# TEAROOM

In southern Korea, the Hadong and Boseong regions have long been celebrated for producing the finest teas, blessed with ideal soil, sunlight, and rainfall. Hadong, nestled between Jirisan Mountain and the Seomjin River, yields young and tender *Jakseol* tea leaves, while Boseong's spring-harvested *Sejak*, kissed by sea breezes and sunshine, is a true delight for tea drinkers. Korean tea, meticulously produced through delicate methods involving small, and tender leaves, naturally embodies an understated charm and mildness.

**Dadore Tearoom**, a small teahouse in Seoul's Yeonhui-dong residential area, is a rare gem dedicated solely to Korean teas. Cho Chaeryeon, who has run Dadore Tearoom for seven years, curated its diverse tea collection by visiting skilled tea farmers nationwide, initially seeking to improve her own health. While seated at Dadore Tearoom's reservation-only tea bar, guests can unwind from the burdens of everyday life. Uniquely, the tea master here also shares the tea with

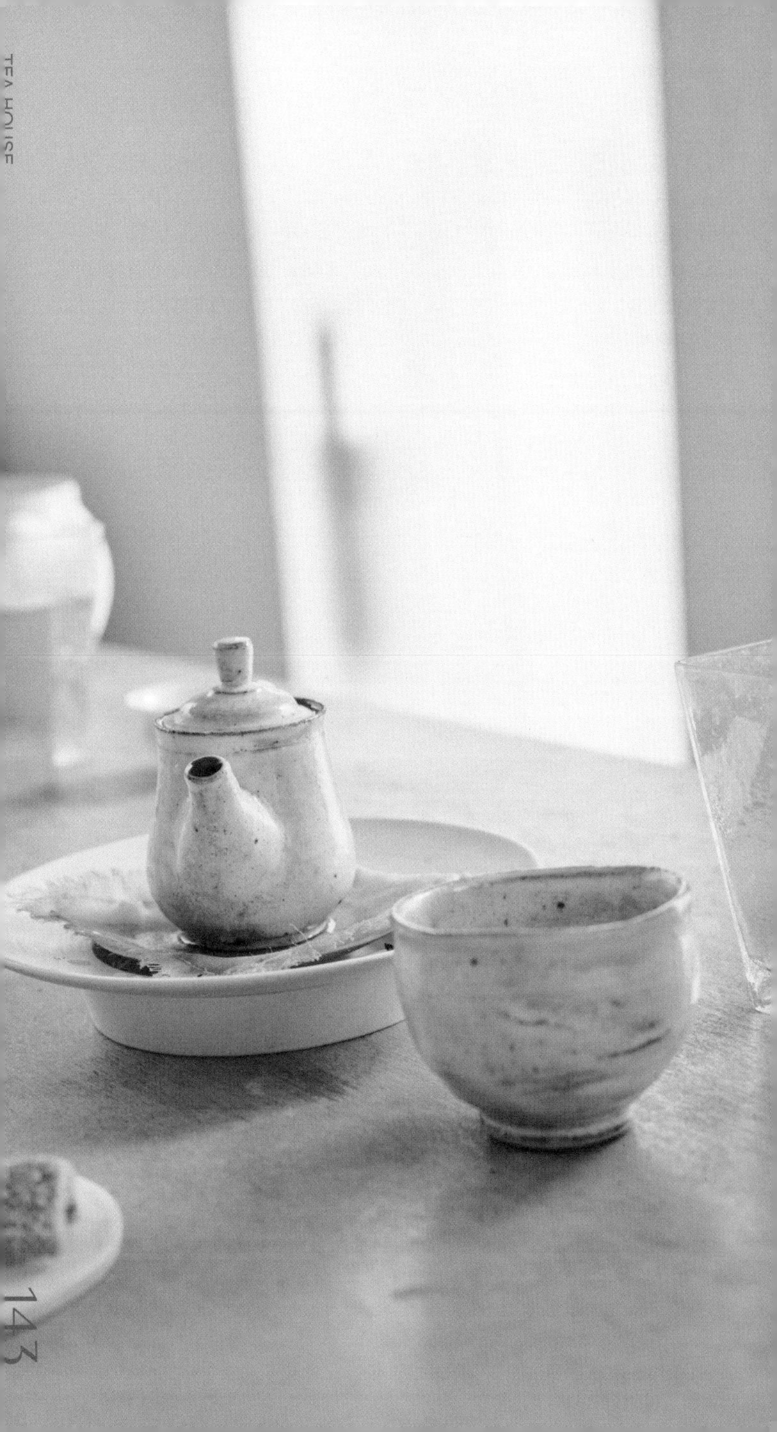

customers, engaging in warm conversation. At Dadore Tearoom, tea is served in exceptionally small portions from tiny *buncheong*-style teapots created in collaboration with ceramist Jang Hunseong. These are so charmingly small that they evoke memories of childhood tea parties. The intention is clear: to encourage the enjoyment of warm tea through multiple infusions, each sip steeped in care and thoughtfulness. The body gradually warms with several cups of the

signature Halmae Ttuium-cha (Grandmother's Fermented Tea). Fermented for a month using traditional *nuruk* (traditional fermentation starter) methods by a lifelong *meju* (fermented soybean blocks) maker, this tea imparts a pleasant bitterness and deep sweetness, warming the body from within. Drinking tea is, in essence, a brief invocation of nature.

    The act of drinking tea is a brief summoning of nature. It is a moment when tea leaves from the plantation meet pure water, steeped and served in teacups crafted by the hands of a ceramist—a sensory ritual that bridges the earth and the body. In this 60-minute experience, brief yet profound, this simple yet extraordinary act might just subtly shift your perspective.

| | |
|---|---|
| DADORE TEAROOM<br>다도레 티룸 | 3F, 13-9, Jeungga-ro, Seodaemun-gu, Seoul<br>@dadore_tea |

# MONGJAE

What kind of place is **Mongjae** (夢齋) meaning "house of dreams"? Nestled on the fourth floor of the annex at **Boan 1942**, a cultural space known for showcasing both the everyday and the avant-garde, Mongjae is a modest tea room of roughly 16.5 square meters. The room's design is intriguing, blurring the lines between indoors and outdoors. Horizontal band windows and a partially retractable roof, held in place by bamboo poles, allow fresh air to circulate freely, creating a subtly shadowy ambiance.

The sole curator of this tea space is its founder, Choi Sungwoo. From tidying the room to preparing the tea and *dasik*[4], to crafting the narratives and atmosphere of the tea gathering itself—every detail is his responsibility This deeply personal approach means Mongjae doesn't operate as a typical teahouse but as an invitation-only private space. To visit, customers must email a brief introduction explaining their intentions and the mindset they bring to the experience. As he

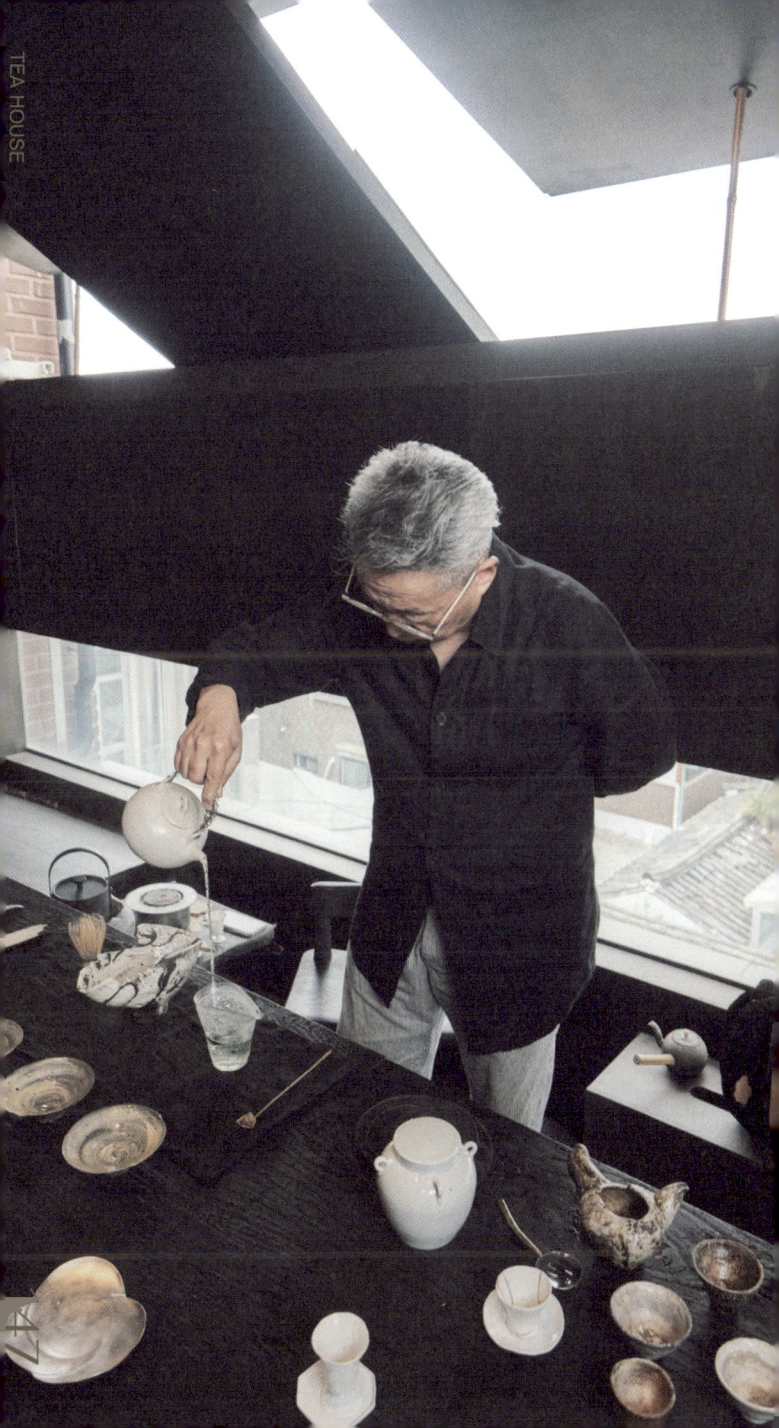

pours Tieguanyin tea from Yunnan into a delicate cup crafted by ceramist Park Sunggeuk, its design reminiscent of folded white *hanji*, he unveils a painting. It is "*Seonyudo*" by Sim Sajeong, a mid-*Joseon* era artist, depicting elderly figures leisurely enjoying a boat ride despite rough waves. It is a favorite of his, reflecting his desire to maintain composure in a turbulent world. Conversations flow naturally over tea, encompassing reflections on life, art, and shared hospitality. These exchanges are punctuated by discussions of different teas and their flavors. A set of *buncheong* ceramics by artisan Eun Sungmin adorns the table. Soon, he begins to whisk powdered tea, creating a white foam reminiscent of matcha, a delicacy once enjoyed by Emperor Huizong of the Song Dynasty.

    I drink a black wolfberry tea, topped with this

white foam, achieved through consistent, rapid whisking that creates swirling patterns in the tea. The aroma, taste, and visual presentation are exquisite, and they evoke a sense of calm rather than excitement. Mongjae feels like a tangible expression of owner Choi Sungwoo's unseen, everyday rhythm—a quiet yet profound world crafted from his unique perspective.

MONGJAE
몽재

4F, 33, Hyoja-ro, Jongno-gu, Seoul
@boan1942.mongjae
summaron79@gmail.com

# CHACHA TEA CLUB BUKCHON LOUNGE

Turning off the bustling Gyedong-gil in Bukchon, a quiet alley reveals a serene *hanok*. This unexpected discovery is delightful enough, but stepping inside reveals something even more special: **Chacha Tea Club Bukchon Lounge**, a sanctuary dedicated to tranquil moments with tea. The *hanok* is built around a courtyard, allowing sunlight and gentle breezes to flow freely through the open rooms and across the wooden floor. The deep amber of the beautifully weathered wooden pillars and the scattering of fallen leaves create a picturesque scene—*hanok* architecture seems to harmonize perfectly with autumn's rich colors.

    Seated on the wooden porch, facing a stone wall adorned with a blooming crape myrtle, I sip the unique "*Minari* Breeze," a blend with a sweet freshness unlike anything I've tasted before. This tea combines the grassy notes of green tea with the subtly bitter taste of water dropwort and kiwi grown in Boseong. Looking up at the aged *seokkarae*[5], I slowly brew "Bai Mu Dan"

(White Peony tea), letting the day's stresses melt away. This tea, from China's Fujian province, features delicate leaves with hints of fresh apple and nutty grains. It is paired with the "Dried Persimmon Salami," a signature *dasik* created by owner Lee Hyunjae. This treat blends dates, figs, pistachios, and almonds, resulting in a delightful chewy yet crisp texture.

My gaze shifts from the flower and charming bird painted on Baegamyo's elegant, milky-white porcelain to the blue sky beyond, each sip of tea adding warmth. The true charm of a tea ceremony lies in this harmonious convergence: the tea's fragrance, the ambiance of the vessel, the natural world just outside, and the anticipation of each new taste. Chacha Tea

Club Bukchon Lounge's appeal extends even further. A small annex behind the *hanok* provides an even more intimate and quiet space, and weekly English tea classes are offered by reservation.

CHACHA TEA CLUB
BUKCHON LOUNGE
차차티클럽 북촌라운지

103-7, Gyedong-gil, Jongno-gu, Seoul
@chacha_willbegood

# DELPHIC ANGUK FLAGSHIP STORE

**Delphic Anguk Flagship Store**, a teahouse in Bukchon, presents an extraordinary and striking visual upon entry—a large, square reflecting pool that guests walk alongside to reach the entrance. As a premium Korean tea brand dedicated to making tea culture accessible, Delphic's Anguk flagship store in Bukchon offers both its signature blended teas and curated artisan exhibitions. The building, a renovated, sturdy 1960s house, was CEO Yoo Sujin's childhood home. Passing through the first-floor gallery and ascending to the second floor, visitors encounter a sunlit tea room—a space that seems to prioritize emptiness over fullness. At the "ㄷ"-shaped tea bar, customers can choose from light, signature blends like "Fig One," "Demeter," or "Artemis," or opt for more robust premium teas such as "Xiaoqinggan," "Tieguanyin," and "Woojeon."

    Among Delphic Anguk Flagship Store's offerings, the herbal tea "Shangri-La" stands out, inspired by the mythical paradise from James Hilton's novel "Lost Horizon." I couldn't help but quietly gasp when this tea was presented. It arrived with ceramist Park Seongwook's *buncheong*-style teapot and double-handled *yangyi* cups, accompanied by snow-white cookies. The ceramic pieces, created by Delphic Anguk Flagship Store in collaboration with various ceramists, perfectly embody the harmony achievable through various shades of white. A sip of "Shangri-La," with its

citrusy blend of lemongrass, fennel, and basil, was followed by a bite of pale green tiramisu, featuring red bean cream layered on a matcha sponge—a perfectly balanced indulgence. Amid this sensory experience, my attention was drawn to the long table displaying various handcrafted items by Korean artisans: teapots, vases, cups, and trays. These carefully selected objects, available for purchase, represent Delphic Anguk Flagship Store's refined aesthetic, seamlessly integrating tea, craft, and space to create an atmosphere of "stillness in time."

    Stepping outside, a narrow iron staircase leads to a small rooftop exhibition space, perched like a lighthouse above the city. From here, the rhythmic undulations of Bukchon's traditional *hanok* rooftops unfold. Beyond them, a panorama of authentic life, spanning centuries past to the present, is framed by Seoul's vast, azure sky.

TEA HOUSE

DELPHIC ANGUK  
FLAGSHIP STORE  
델픽 안국 플래그십 스토어

2F, 84-3, Gyedong-gil, Jongno-gu, Seoul  
@delphic_official

# A D O
# GYEYOUNGBAE

On the fifth floor of the ARGO Building is teahouse **Ado Gyeyoungbae**. Originally established in Mullae-dong, this is Ado Gyeyoungbae's second location, opened in 2024. With its low ceiling, the space feels cozy, like a bar tucked under the eaves. While carefully peeling a perfectly ripe persimmon, owner Lee Seungwoo asks, "How are you feeling today?" True to its name, which means "the path to oneself," Ado Gyeyoungbae's curates teas matched to seven different emotions, serving a tea that corresponds to your current state of mind. This is his approach to tea therapy, born from his desire to listen to customers' stories and offer comfort.

As I openly share my recent experiences, he pauses thoughtfully before expertly brewing a cup of tea. It's Yueming Chachang, a fermented tea harvested in 1998 in Yunnan, China. The tea, with its deep color and almost medicinal depth, reflects the decades it has aged. Drinking this tea, enhanced by its taste, aroma,

and emotional resonance, I feel an immediate lift in spirits. The abstract, painting-like brushstrokes on the wall opposite the bar are actually created by customers using lacquer—another of the owner's ideas, encouraging them to "Express their current emotions without reservation." This evolving mural is becoming Ado Gyeyoungbae's most distinctive feature. Furthermore, Ado Gyeyoungbae is beautifully adorned with bonsai trees—*Rhus succedanea* (wax tree) and *Juniperus chinensis* 'Itoigawa' (Itoigawa juniper). Though small, each species displays a unique form and captivating color. An old stone brazier heats water, while carefully selected stones, chosen by his discerning eye, rest on the tables. Surrounded by bonsai, viewing stones, and tea, we naturally share a sense of warmth while discussing "nature's forms," much like the literary scholars of old. Meanwhile, the teacups in my hands, crafted by ceramists Kim Eungchul and Ahn Changho, reveal their pristine beauty as they are filled and emptied.

ADO GYEYOUNGBAE  
아도 계영배

5F, 16, Eonju-ro 173-gil, Gangnam-gu, Seoul  
@a.do.official

# E  E  U  M

Upon entering **eeum**, customers immediately sense a heartfelt dedication in every meticulously arranged detail, from the teaware to the pristine white tea cloths. The serene atmosphere is imbued with the daily ritual of owner Joo Myunghee, who begins each day with a renewed spirit, placing a vessel of pure water by the window and lighting a candle as soon as she opens the teahouse. eeum takes its name from the residence of *Joseon*-era literary scholar Jang Hon, who lived in Okryu-dong and found joy in nature. Okryu-dong is the former name of Okin-dong, where eeum is now located. Inspired by Jang Hon's self-sufficient life of appreciating tea and poetry with friends, Joo established her own haven here seven years ago.

   Eeum primarily showcases Taiwanese Oolong, Chinese Wuyi rock tea, and Korean yellow and green teas. The space also hosts five to six exhibitions annually, featuring craft artists whose work resonates with eeum's tranquil and pure aesthetic. The tearoom

TEA HOUSE

167

is closed during exhibitions, otherwise, reservations are required at least one day in advance. White is the dominant color at eeum, extending from the white walls to the meticulously handcrafted camellia and plum blossoms made from white *hanji* by craft artist So Hosoo. At the heart of the tearoom, a white brazier with a steaming kettle further enhances the atmosphere. At that moment, Joo Myunghee carefully places *Muzha Tieguanyin* tea leaves, prized for their distinctive charcoal-roasted flavor, into a small *buncheong* teapot.

At eeum, the owner Joo personally demonstrates the art of brewing and pouring tea, patiently guiding customers on the amount of tea leaves to use and how to comfortably hold the teapot. As the tea flows into my body, I feel a sense of mental cleansing. Later, I lingered in the deeply gathered light and quiet but was soon brought back to the present by the chiming of a pendulum clock. eeum remains in my memory as one of Seoul's most serene places.

TEA HOUSE

EEUM
이이엄

3, Pirundae-ro 9-gil, Jongno-gu, Seoul
@_eeum

# 1994
# SEOUL

In Korea, *Jeolgi*[6] is a unique way of dividing the year into seasons. Ancestors divided the year into 24 solar terms, planning agricultural activities, culinary traditions, and fully appreciating nature's beauty during each term. **1994SEOUL** is a teahouse that offers a modern experience of this fading cultural heritage, allowing visitors to connect with *jeolgi* through tea and *byeonggwa* (traditional Korean confections). The year "1994" in the name holds dual significance for owner Lee Myungjae: it represents both his birth year and the year his parents established a rice cake shop in Incheon. Honoring his parents' three decades of dedication, he opened 1994SEOUL in Yeonnam-dong. Here, he continually explores traditional teas and confections suited to *jeolgi* and *sesipungsok*[7]. He introduces seasonal tea courses, aligned with the solar terms, about five to six times a year, personally serving each menu item and sharing its story.

    As the end of September approaches, marking

*chubun*[8]—a time when day and night are of equal length—autumn is just around the corner. Around this time, guests can enjoy a delicately blended persimmon leaf tea infused with pumpkin, red bean, and adlay. The sweet and savory aroma of chrysanthemum *bukkumi*—pan-fried rice cakes with white red bean filling and perilla oil—naturally evokes the essence of the season. The delicate flower petals imprinted on the white *bukkumi* come from wild autumn chrysanthemums. As the full flavor of autumn unfolds on the palate and through the senses, a small *yakgwa*—a traditional honey cookie—is retrieved from a *Joseon* Dynasty *najeonchilgi*[9] box. 1994SEOUL's signature *yakgwa*, with its delightful chewy texture and a harmonious blend of ginger and the sweetness of *jocheong* (rice syrup), recalls the taste of homemade treats lovingly prepared by a grandmother.

    As three varieties of tea and eight exquisite confections grace the table, the tactile experience of encountering special treasures—teaware such as a teapot and teacup crafted by ceramic artisan Yoo Taegeun, a lacquered *daha* (tea table) by master woodworker Choi Seongwoo, and even a triple-tiered white porcelain box from the *Joseon* era—creates a sensory journey that transports you to a Seoul existing only in that moment.

1994SEOUL
1994서울

20-12, Seongmisan-ro 23an-gil, Mapo-gu, Seoul
@1994seoul_official

# CHACHAITHÉ

Chachaithé combines three words meaning tea: "cha (茶)," "chai," and "thé." Stepping into **Chachaithé**, tucked away in a quiet alley beyond Itaewon's bustle, feels like arriving in a neutral space devoid of coordinates. Inside the tearoom, past a small antechamber that refreshes the spirit, sits an L-shaped bar table with rounded corners accompanied by six Thonet chairs. Guests are seated by reservation in this intimate space, where brief, pleasant greetings are the only exchanges between those who come for a special tea moment.

The tea journey begins with lemon myrtle grown in Naju, Jeollanam-do. As Chachaithé is a teahouse inspired by tea confectionery, guests can anticipate beautiful and sweet *dasik* that perfectly complement the blended teas. The "Monaka Florentine" topped with roasted sesame seeds, the delicately crumbling "Vanilla Viennois," and the "Fig and Blue Cheese Tart" with its exquisite-tasting white bean paste truly mark the

pinnacle of the experience. These three confections, which either melt instantly or offer a dense crunch, pair perfectly with a sip of the luscious Osmanthus Go-Yom tea made from roasted persimmon leaves. The ever-changing teas, sweets, and tableware with each season naturally leave you anticipating your next tea time at Chachaithé. The space's oriental yet futuristic ambiance is attributed to the unique coloration of metal used in the sliding doors, tables, and ceiling lights. This remarkable result was created through a collaboration between interior designer Lim Taehee of Lim Taehee Design Studio and metal craftsman Kim Donggyu. Overall, the place showcases a subdued metallic aesthetic using matte aluminum that never feels overpowering. Ceramist Park Sunggeuk's small square plates, resembling folded *hanji*, Kim Donggyu's octagonal silver trays and forks, and even the coral spoon rest—all exude Chachaithé's distinct craft-oriented taste.

After a thoroughly satisfying tea experience, I purchased boxes of Vanilla Viennois and candied walnuts from the shop just across from the tearoom. As I stepped outside, a refreshing breeze brushed against my neck—it felt as light as the paper bag in my hand.

CHACHAITHÉ
차차이테

74, Itaewon-ro 54-gil, Yongsan-gu, Seoul
@chachaithe

# MAGPIE &
# TIGER SINSA
# TEAROOM

*"We roasted and toasted the leftover stems from making green tea. Perhaps the desire to not waste a single stem is contained within each cup."* This heartfelt message is printed on the *hojicha* tea card at **Magpie&Tiger Sinsa Tearoom**. Here, each tea is introduced not by its benefits or functions, but through evocative descriptions of its aroma, color, and the weather it best complements. This charming approach brings a smile and a moment of reflection when choosing a tea. Magpie&Tiger offers a relaxed exploration of East Asian teas, from Chinese varieties like Yunnan white tea and Yiwu, 2012 Ripe Puer Tea to Korean teas such as Hadong *Jackseol* Tea, mugwort tea, and burdock root tea.

    I stepped past a white shade into the dimly lit tearoom, illuminated by soft beams of light, and settled into a quiet space. At the center of the long black tea bar, hot water simmered in a copper kettle. The seasonal autumn tea course begins with caffeine-free,

toasty pumpkin tea, gently warming the body. Between sips of *Jakseol* tea, notable for its fresh tomato stem aroma, I enjoyed a tart topped with glazed chestnuts. The "*hojicha* highball"—a creative combination of sparkling *hojicha* and whiskey—is a distinctive offering at Magpie&Tiger. The golden line at the rim of the clear porcelain cup I drink from, crafted by Torim Ceramics, reflects the artistry of ceramist Lee Eunbi's kintsugi work, a traditional Japanese ceramic repair technique. This Japanese technique of repairing broken pottery with gold embodies the passage of time and the preciousness of objects. Magpie&Tiger's name is inspired by "*Hojakdo*," traditional Korean folk paintings depicting magpies and tigers as symbols of good fortune and well-being. True to its name, the

tearoom invites you to savor tea as we appreciate art in daily life. Located on the second floor of a Garosu-gil alley in Gangnam, this space maintains a serene yet welcoming atmosphere, both refined and intimate. Even for those visiting alone, the tea becomes a comforting companion.

MAGPIE&TIGER
SINSA TEAROOM
맥파이앤타이거 신사 티룸

2F, 44, Nonhyeon-ro 153-gil, Gangnam-gu, Seoul
@magpie.and.tiger

# OSULLOC TEA HOUSE BUKCHON

Osulloc, Korea's premier tea brand, sources its leaves from its own lush plantations on Jeju Island. The brand's story began in 1979, when the barren, rocky Jeju inland was transformed into verdant tea fields. Nestled in Jeju's serene embrace, **Osulloc Tea House Bukchon** is more than just a tea house—it is a sensory ode to Korean traditions. This space allows guests to experience a wide selection of teas, Korean tradition-inspired desserts, and the synesthetic essence of Korean sensibilities. Housed in a renovated 1960s Western-style building, the teahouse welcomes customers with a garden of *Potentilla fruticosa*, *Cornus kousa*, and vibrant pink flowers. This naturally guides them inside.

The interior is divided into distinct rooms—Tea Atelier on the first floor, Tea Lounge on the second floor, and Tea Room on the third floor— capturing the comfort of being a guest in someone's home. This thoughtful layout allows guests to choose their

preferred seating, and on pleasant days, the terrace offers a mountain lodge-like atmosphere. The teapots used to brew *sejak* tea, known for its delicate leaves, are crafted by ceramist Ji Seungmin and possess a texture and color that are as rough and unassuming as Jeju stones. The glass teapots for iced tea, featuring chunky handles resembling Jeju stones, are exclusively designed for Osulloc by Grigo Glass Studio using the glassblowing technique.

Their innovative dessert plate, Bukchon's *Saekdong*, presents multiple layers of Korean flavors with grilled rice cakes and four colorful dipping sauces. It is a satisfyingly substantial offering, combining the chewy texture of seaweed-wrapped *garaetteok* (long-shaped rice cake) and Jeju *gijeongtteok* (also known as *jeung-pyun*, a rice wine-fermented rice cake) with the spiciness of red pepper jam and the sweetness of green tangerine syrup.

On the third floor, Bar Sulloc evokes the vibe of a 1960s retro bar. It is the perfect place to enjoy sophisticated mocktails such as the "Volcanic Hallatini" or the "Tangerine Bukchon Sling" while taking in views of Bukchon's landscape, where past and present intertwine. Across from the bar, the Tea Room becomes a private space when its white *hanji* doors are closed. A special tea course is held daily, featuring the changing seasons of Jeju and the diverse stories of Osulloc teas. Reservations are essential for those seeking this immersive experience, accompanied only by the gentle sound of pouring water.

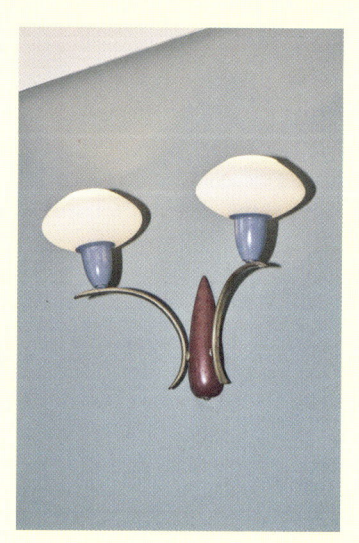

OSULLOC TEA HOUSE
BUKCHON
오설록 티하우스 북촌

45, Bukchon-ro, Jongno-gu, Seoul
@osulloc_official

# O M O T

**OMOT**, a teahouse nestled in Seongsu-dong, offers a warm, immersive tea experience within its dark, metallic-toned space. The name "OMOT" carries a dual meaning: "On My Own Time" and "Out of Many, Our Tea." Drawing from tea journeys across Korea, founder/CEO Kim Hyejin and Kim Yonghyun personally curate over 30 varieties of tea that they blend themselves, including *Geumryu*, *Gamip*, *Ssukro*, *Hwangchil*, *and Jaeksal*. In particular, the tea ceremony at OMOT invites you to focus deeply on the artistry of tea-making, the care behind each blend, and the craftsmanship of Korean artisans. Each year, the ceremony evolves around themes rooted in traditional Korean culture, such as the four seasons, 24 *jeolgi*, 12 zodiac animals, and the *sipjangsaeng*. Within the dimly lit space, a sheer black silk gauze curtain subtly demarcates the bar where courses are enjoyed from the seating for those casually sipping teas.

    You begin your tea journey with a welcome tea,

a black *Hwangchil* leaf tea served in a cocktail glass rimmed with vanilla syrup and pepper, as CEO Kim Hyejin's gentle explanation draws you into the day's experience. The "*Haejachugin*" (亥子丑寅) ceremony, representing pig, rat, ox, and tiger, commences with a sip of *Saemon* tea, a blend of ginger and lemongrass that warms the body. In a celadon-green *gyeyeongbae* cup made by Dajeong Ceramics—designed to spill if filled past 70%—tea is poured with the message of moderation and humility. A spontaneous brushstroke on a cup by ceramist Ro Jeongyo, inspired by Korean modernist painter Lee Jungseob's iconic white ox, is paired with a North Korean-style *injeolmi*, evoking the ox's energetic spirit. The taste, color, and texture of each tea shift subtly depending on the vessel used—one of the hidden pleasures of the ceremony. Even the accompanying soundtrack, created in collaboration with traditional Korean musicians, guides you into a meditative state throughout the 90-minute experience of tea and *dasik*.

OMOT  
오므오트

B1F, 12, Seoulsup 2-gil, Seongdong-gu, Seoul  
@_omot_

# T O V E

Wandering around Anguk Station, I'm struck by the subtle interplay of different atmospheres. On one side lies Insa-dong, steeped in tradition with antique art, vintage furniture, and rare books. Across the street, Bukchon unfolds with a contemporary cultural vibe, boasting museums, galleries, and parks. When torn between these two distinct worlds, I invariably find myself drawn to **TOVE** for a cup of tea.

Climbing to the third floor of a building on the way into Insa-dong, I'm greeted by large windows that frame a vibrant scene: a tree outside, its branches swaying gently in the breeze, ablaze with autumn's fiery foliage. The name "TOVE" comes from the Chinese word for "special (特別)." Tea director Lee Sehee, inspired by her time living in Guangzhou, where tea is an integral part of even the simplest meals, was deeply impressed by the everyday presence of tea in Chinese culture. This experience shaped TOVE's vibrant and unconventional atmosphere, setting it

apart from more traditional teahouses. To create this unique ambiance, she collaborated with the brand CAA, incorporating black, white, and red metal tables and shelves, creating a space where young people can enjoy tea in their own way.

What does tea taste like in a setting reminiscent of De Stijl, with its bold colors and geometric lines? Among the selection of oolong, white, and black teas, the signature "Tove Oolong" stands out for its creamy, smooth profile. The refreshing "Homemade Lemon Jelly," served atop bright lemon peel, is another must-try. The round, asymmetrical teacups and plates are the work of ceramist Jo Heejin, who runs the ceramic craft brands Night Fruity and the ceramic studio Eastsmoke, adding depth and richness to TOVE's visual landscape.

TOVE also is popular with international tourists, so a short wait is sometimes necessary. However, this time can be pleasantly spent exploring Korean crafts at the Seoul Museum of Craft Art, located just across the street, making the anticipated tea experience even more rewarding.

TOVE
토오베

3F, 62-4, Insadong-gil, Jongno-gu, Seoul
@room.tove

DIN

| | |
|---|---|
| 204 | ONJIUM RESTAURANT |
| 210 | MINGLES |
| 216 | JUNGSIK SEOUL |
| 222 | THE GREEN TABLE |
| 228 | RESTAURANT JUEUN |
| 234 | EVETT |
| 240 | RESTAURANT ALLEN |
| 246 | SOLBAM |
| 252 | KWONSOOKSOO |
| 258 | SOSEOUL HANNAM |
| 264 | GIWAKANG |
| 270 | LA YEON |
| 276 | BICENA |

# ING

# ONJIUM
# RESTAURANT

**Onjium Restaurant** offers exceptional Korean fine-dining that revitalizes traditional cuisine with contemporary flavors and aesthetics. Inspired by the *Joseon*-era *banga*[1] cuisine of the noble class, Onjium Restaurant reinterprets these dishes using contemporary ingredients and techniques, creating an unparalleled culinary journey. The restaurant's panoramic views of *Gyeongbokgung* Palace, Inwangsan Mountain, and Bukaksan Mountain at a glance is a spectacle comparable to the taste. it allows you to feel the changing seasons of Seoul every moment.

The menu, updated every two months, tells a unique story projected by Korea's finest seasonal ingredients, weather, and colors. Over nine meticulously crafted courses, diners are treated to a narrative-like progression of flavors and visuals. Onjium Restaurant's dedication to tradition is evident in its house-made condiments like soy sauce, vinegar, *doenjang* (soybean paste), and *gochujang* (red pepper

paste), as well as its carefully prepared broths. Led by Culinary Director Cho Eunhee and Head Chef Park Sungbae, a team of thirteen staff members works seamlessly in the glass enclosed kitchen in passionate synchronization. The meal begins with elegant bites like tofu wedges, *gamtae* crisps, steamed lotus root and *haseol yugwa* served on handcrafted blue plates by ceramist Lee Heonjeong. The cold "Seafood & Beef Kimchi Salad" of abalone, baby octopus, and beef delivers a distinctive umami, while the steamboat dish "*Yeolgujatang*"—a delicate slice of minced beef, lamb,

pheasant, abalone, and king prawns—lives up to its name as a dish that delights the palate. Onjium Restaurant's a natural and simple yet elegant plating literally permeates the historical idiom "儉而不陋 華而不侈," which means that it is simple but not shabby, and luxurious but not extravagant.

ONJIUM RESTAURANT  
온지음 레스토랑

4F, 49, Hyoja-ro, Jongno-gu, Seoul,  
@onjium_restaurant

# MINGLES

Stepping into **Mingles**, you immediately feel embraced by an atmosphere that soothes all your senses. The large arched windows, the fine-grained wooden floors, the royal palace picture by photographer Kim Heewon adorning the walls, and the understated beauty of *dalhangari* and vases with attractive flowers, all come together to create the unique charm of Mingles. True to its name, this is a place where ingredients, cooking methods, culture, craftsmanship, and experiences harmonize seamlessly. Celebrating its eleventh anniversary this year since 2014, Chef Kang Mingoo's quiet yet powerful passion has marked a milestone in the restaurant's history with its recognition as a Michelin 3-star establishment in 2025. The 13-course menu, which respects Korean traditional cuisine while incorporating contemporary sensibilities and techniques, is enough to spark genuine excitement.

    The first course presents a delightful contrast of simplicity and sophistication with a small piece of

potato *injeolmi* (sticky rice cake), a warm chestnut soup topped with truffle, and a strawberry delicately garnished with caviar. Next comes the restaurant's signature dish, "Mingling Pot," served in a cream-colored bowl crafted by ceramist Moon Dain. Inside are three types of dumplings, abalone, pan-fried lotus root, and sea cucumber, all gently steeped in a pale anchovy broth—nourishing and deeply soothing. A sticky rice risotto topped with king crab, tomato, and mussels offers a savory richness that speaks of time and patience. Mingles' elegance shines through its plating—modest yet showing deliberate articulation with careful control of subtle dynamics. A standout example is the roulade—served on a round plate by ceramist Park Seoyeon—where each ingredient is placed like four points in a composition. The crispy yet tender texture of the chicken, paired with burdock pickles, ginseng meatballs, and black vinegar sauce, shows a remarkable sense of balance.

As the course nears its end, the dessert "*Jang* Trio" takes center stage. Featuring *doenjang* crème brûlée, soy sauce pecans, and *gochujang* puffed rice, this dish encapsulates Mingles' essence. It reflects Chef Kang Mingoo's deep affection for Korean fermented sauces, as seen in his book "*Jang*." The dessert blends sweet, salty, and spicy flavors into a harmonious finale. If you're seeking modern Korean fine dining where taste and aesthetics converge beautifully, remember the charming name Mingles.

MINGLES  
밍글스

2F, 19, Dosan-daero 67-gil, Gangnam-gu, Seoul  
@mingles_restaurant

# JUNGSIK
# SEOUL

**JUNGSIK SEOUL**, a pioneer of New Korean fine dining with locations in both Seoul and New York, has redefined the Korean gastronomy field. In December 2024, JUNGSIK in Tribeca, New York, earned a Michelin 3-star rating, praised for its precise and sophisticated harmony of flavors. This achievement marked a historic milestone as the first Korean fine dining restaurant in the United States to receive such an honor. Head Chef Im Jungsik of JUNGSIK SEOUL is known for adding both wit and elegance to inventive dishes rooted in everyday Korean cuisine, rather than relying on excessive reinterpretation. His clever elevation of familiar dishes like *gimbap* and *naengmyeon* into refined culinary creations, along with his use of *kimchi* to balance acidity in dishes, clearly reflects this unique approach.

    The original JUNGSIK, located in Cheongdam-dong, opened in 2009 and quickly became a cornerstone of Seoul's fine-dining scene. Its interior

design features blue velvet chairs, pin lighting focused on plates, and objects inspired by traditional *tteoksal* (traditional rice cake mold) patterns, embodying contemporary Seoul. The first course, named "*Banchan*," is a dazzling start. Small bites such as foie-gras tartlets, smoked mackerel, *yukhoe* (Korean beef tartare) toast, and tofu dipped in perilla oil are arranged like miniature works of art on a white ceramic cube, creating a rhythmic visual display. This flavorful array is further enhanced by the *gimbap* that follows, showcased on a pristine white plate. Rolled with scallops and mullet roe, the *gimbap* is accompanied by sweet shrimp, squid sashimi, grilled *deodeok* (mountain root), and caviar arranged like a painter's palette. The crispy texture of *gimbugak* (fried seaweed chips) and the joy of customizing with seven side pairings add layers of delight. The amplified expression of seasonality is another hallmark of JUNGSIK SEOUL. Grilled tilefish served in a green *maesaengi* (fine seaweed) broth alongside northern clams and oyster dumplings carries the full essence of the ocean. The culinary journey concludes with a dessert that transports you to Korea's remote islands—a *dolharubang* (grandfather stone statue in Jeju) inspired creation. Reminiscent of Jeju Island's volcanic formations, this pistachio dessert replicates the rough texture of basalt stone while featuring maple syrup made from Ulleungdo *gorosoe* sap. Gently breaking open a pistachio *dolharubang* with its stubby nose and gentle smile using a fork, scattering the crumble, and placing it in your mouth alongside lemon sorbet is an act as intense and delightful as an adventure to a distant island.

JUNGSIK SEOUL
정식당

11, Seolleung-ro 158-gil, Gangnam-gu, Seoul
@jungsik_inc

# THE GREEN TABLE

**The Green Table**, located on the fifth floor of a building in Wonseo-dong, offers spectacular views of Changdeokgung Palace. With floor-to-ceiling windows on three sides, it presents Seoul's most picturesque scenery during the day and creates an otherworldly dining experience at night, as if floating in space. Owner-chef Kim Eunhee, who has led The Green Table for 16 years, is highly respected by her peers for her culinary expertise and relentless pursuit of excellence. Although she began her career in French cuisine, she returned to Korea to study temple and royal court cooking, and spent years traveling across the country to explore seasonal ingredients. This dedication is one reason her Korean-French cuisine is so beloved.

The meal begins with four amuse-bouches: butternut squash soup, raw shrimp topped with *gamtae*, a tart with finely chopped pistachio and cream cheese, and torch-grilled pear. They make a gorgeous first impression on the table. Each beautiful dish, working as a canvas for food, is served on handcrafted plates made by Korean ceramists. Especially notable is the soup bowl by Kim Heejong, which bears the engraved Chinese character "福" (fortune), conveying wishes for health and luck.

The breathtaking "Summer Garden salad" features young farm leaves with zucchini-mint purée, dressed with champagne, evoking morning dew on green leaves. Such outstanding summer scenes remain a constant theme in The Green Table's repertoire throughout the year.

Next comes a dish of black grains with slowly grilled lotus root on rice made with black barley and oats, followed by white abalone dumplings filled with minced fermented bamboo shoots and Korean beef, served in radish and beef consommé. The progression from the dark grains to the delicate white abalone dumplings creates a lively contrast in both color and flavor, moving from rich and hearty to light and refined. The signature "Five Pickles"—Sichuan pepper sprouts, Jerusalem artichoke, ginseng, Coastal Hog Fennel, and Korean Meadow Rue leaves—arranged on a white plate, look like an ink painting. Ultimately, The Green Table's sophisticated seasonal cuisine, combined with its stunning views, creates an unforgettable dining experience where the landscape on the plate seamlessly connects with the scenery beyond the windows.

THE GREEN TABLE
더그린테이블

5F, 83, Yulgok-ro, Jongno-gu, Seoul
@restaurant_thegreentable

# RESTAURANT JUEUN

Just as various foods are brought together in a single *hap* (porcelain containers with a lid), **Restaurant Jueun** gathers exceptional layers of Korea's seasons and traditions into a refined and cohesive culinary experience. Led by Chef Park Jueun, the restaurant introduces a modern Korean dining concept deeply rooted in traditional cuisine. By presenting the pure flavors of ingredients with clarity and intuition, Restaurant Jueun offers an authentic Korean course that reflects the life and soul of the Korean people—infused with the chef's own unique flair. To achieve this, the menu features a complete *hansang* (a collection of different dishes) that harmoniously blends rice, soup, *namul* (seasoned vegetables), and *kimchi*—the cornerstones of Korean cuisine—while steadfastly adhering to tradition by excluding Western ingredients like cream, butter, and caviar. This commitment is recognized in the diverse use of tableware crafted by Korean artisans, such as celadon, *buncheong* ware,

earthenware, black pottery, and woodenware, in each course.

Located in Gwanghwamun, the historic heart of Seoul, Restaurant Jueun features elegant negative space between the *hanji*-finished walls and tables. On three large wall panels, dynamic media art by artist Jung Jaejin unfolds—blending imagery of landscapes, ceramics, *dancheong*[2] patterns, and Korean script. In the two private rooms, designer Jang Eungbok's white porcelain-patterned wallpaper and shades, alongside fabric motifs inspired by Korean heritage, add subtle sophistication.

While admiring the vibrantly blooming double cherry blossoms, *Hanipgeori* (a collection of bite-sized delicacies) arrives in a white *hap* decorated with plum blossoms by ceramist Park Byungho. This amuse-bouche set includes steamed buns made of buckwheat and *makgeolli*, yellowtail rolls wrapped in ripened kimchi with sansho pepper, beef tartare topped with pear, and fragrant kohlrabi marinated in honey and pine nut powder with seaweed—each bite awakening your palate. A cold *naengchae* salad, artfully arranged with patterned squid and seaweed, delivers a refreshing tang and visual charm reminiscent of *jogakbo* (traditional patchwork). The subsequent plate brings savory aromas with charcoal-grilled abalone and assorted mushrooms—hen-of-the-woods, black, and *neungi*—combined in *japchae*, leaving a lingering impression through the harmony of varied textures and the aroma of perilla oil and toasted sesame seeds. Restaurant Jueun concludes its courses with traditional Korean desserts that are now rare even in Korea: floral punches, *hwajeon* (flower rice pancakes), and *gangjeong* (crispy sweet rice puffs), offering a perfectly graceful ending to a deeply rooted and thoughtful meal.

RESTAURANT JUEUN
레스토랑 주은

8F, 36, Gyeonghuigung-gil, Jongno-gu, Seoul
@jueun_restaurant

# EVETT

As a Michelin two-star restaurant, **EVETT** has created Korean contemporary fine-dining with natural colors and flavors. The name of the restaurant is a middle name of Joseph Lidgerwood, the Australian chef who is charge of this place. He traveled around the world, exploring ingredients and building culinary experience. Eventually, he decided to make Seoul his gastronomic home after visiting Korea for a pop-up and opened EVETT in 2018. The expectation from Koreans about his Korean contemporary presentation is both an energy and a stimulus to him as a foreign chef. EVETT's originality is to challenge Korean ingredients and cooking methods without any preconceptions or limitations and reinterpret them into gourmet and aesthetics. Much like his childhood in Tasmania, Lidgerwood immerses himself in Korea's deepest mountains, forests, and seas, discovering ingredients unfamiliar even to locals—*Bawiot* (rock seaweed), cabbage root, and perilla frutescens. Moreover, his

plating is equally daring, incorporating delicate petals, branches, and even traditional earthenware jars to create dramatic tablescapes.

EVETT's menu is also a narrative-driven experience, with 14 thematic keywords such as "wild," "focus," and "exploration" replacing traditional dish names. Each course unveils a vivid connection to nature and seasonality. Poached oysters topped with white cream burst with acidity and creamy texture, while rock seaweed jelly dressed with gardenia sauce, celtuce pickles, and fried salted shrimp delivers the ocean's distinctive briny freshness. The natural sensory journey intensifies. On the wooden plate by wood craftswoman Kim Songee, who expressed Baekdusan Mountain with mother-of-pearl inlay, cabbage root slices surround the grilled chopped cabbage root like lotus petals. The main course features smoked Korean

beef steak accompanied by slow-simmered burdock root purée sauce, striking across the plate like an intense ink brushstroke. Like this, EVETT offers not just exceptional cuisine but also chef Joseph Lidgerwood's own experiences, refined yet wild expressions, and boundless imagination.

EVETT
에빗

1F, 10-5, Dosan-daero 45-gil, Gangnam-gu, Seoul
@restaurantevett

# RESTAURANT ALLEN

At **Restaurant Allen,** each course transforms Korea's seasonal ingredients into expressions of flavor and aroma, beautifully capturing the country's four distinct seasons through food. Chef Allen Suh, whose 17 years in the U.S. shaped his hybrid identity, brings dishes that bridge Korean roots and global influences. After honing his skills at New York's Michelin 3-star **Eleven Madison Park**, he opened Restaurant Allen in 2021 with a vision to pioneer Korean-French cuisine. The restaurant's interior, designed by **Areaplus**—renowned for blending artisanal elements with modern aesthetics—features walnut as its foundation, accented by copper, traditional *hanji*, and enamel-glazed lighting. This craftsmanship extends to partitions made from antique wood, wall tiles resembling the texture of *hanji*, and sculptural lines intersecting vertically and horizontally to create a harmonious flow.

      On the back of Restaurant Allen's menu, a map details the origins of each ingredient used. Before the course begins, a box containing the season's featured ingredients is presented to you—a thoughtful performance that sets the tone for what's to come. The restaurant's dedication to seasonal Korean produce is matched by its seamless integration of Western luxuries like truffles and lobster. This combination defines Restaurant Allen's cuisine as both distinctive and deeply creative. One standout amuse-

bouche, the *dureup* (Fatsia Shoot) *tart*, features blanched shoots of Korean angelica nestled in a tartlet shell, lightly grilled over charcoal to draw out their earthy taste and evoke the scent of spring. A warm dish that follows balances the richness of snow crab with soft egg custard, and roasted baby napa cabbage. Then comes a seafood medley—whelk, scallop, and sweet shrimp—each plump and flavorful, embraced by a Jeju citrus sauce and presented on understated ceramic ware crafted by ceramist Lee Songam. Restaurant Allen's courses, with their mysterious harmony of flavor, texture, and body, reflect Chef Suh's final touch—a chef who loves the art of Picasso, Andy Warhol, and Kim Whanki. Furthermore, the dynamic activity of the kitchen team, occupying half the restaurant's space, and the experienced yet welcoming hospitality of the front-of-house team transform the time spent into both an immersive experience and a phenomenal memory.

RESTAURANT ALLEN
레스토랑 알렌

2F, Center field EAST E205, 231, Teheran-ro,
Gangnam-gu, Seoul
@restaurant_allen

# SOLBAM

Upon entering **SOLBAM**, you first encounter an unexpectedly dim space. The cave-like low ceiling and the pulsing rhythm of funky music in the lounge create a moody atmosphere that quickly transforms initial anticipation into joyful intrigue. Seated in what's called the Drawing Room, you begin your experience with a welcome dish presented in a wooden gift box tied with a green ribbon. A light tasting of swordtip squid marinated in lemon soy sauce and a mousse of *doenjang* chicken liver sets the tone before guests are ushered into the main dining area to begin the full course.

As the space brightens dramatically—like stepping into another world—your senses are awakened. SOLBAM, a restaurant that feels like a complete work of art, captivates with its museum-like saturation and textures, large paintings adorning the walls, and the bustling activity of the open kitchen team.

Opened in 2021 by Chef Eom Taejun, SOLBAM crafts neo-classic Korean cuisine rooted in Korea's

unique *terroir*. The restaurant's name, derived from "Solbam Village" in Andong—Chef Eom's pine tree-filled hometown—captures warm lyricism and lingering emotional resonance. His commitment to elevating cuisine to an art form unfolds over a meticulously orchestrated three-hour dining experience. Collaborations with ceramists' art works, such as Min Seunggi's elegant plates and Jeon Sanggeun's fermented sauce vessels shaped like traditional cauldrons, further enhance the visual and tactile pleasure of the meal. A standout dish of perilla oil-covered smoked mackerel mixed with pickled quail eggs served atop crispy *gimbugak* bursts with luscious, pleasantly acidic notes. When something more substantial is desired, the sirloin steak, accompanied by burdock pickles and *deodeok* salad that embody the minerals of the winter earth, fills the palate with its tender texture and sweet aroma. A hidden dish not on the menu, the *Hanwoo* (Korean beef) *noodles*, offers the enjoyment of personally selecting one favorite from six different wooden chopsticks pairs. Moreover, the chosen pair used during the meal are presented to you as a gift. Adding subtle sensibility to top-tier cuisine with a clear theme is the most remarkable dedication that SOLBAM achieves.

SOLBAM  
솔밤

2F, 231, Hakdong-ro, Gangnam-gu, Seoul  
@solbam_restaurant

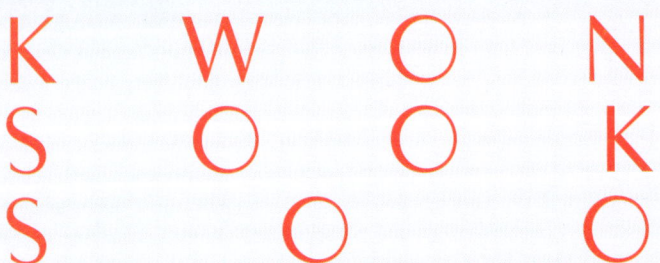

# KWONSOOKSOO

The passionate culinary DNA that runs through owner-Chef Kwon Woojoong of **Kwonsooksoo** originated from his maternal family. His grandfather, who ran a restaurant specializing in North Korean cuisine, and his mother, who skillfully made dumplings and *jokbal* (braised pig's trotters) at home, passed down a strong legacy of Korean cooking that built his 25-year career. Kwonsooksoo, a Michelin 2-star fine-dining restaurant, showcases traditional Korean cuisine reimagined for the modern era using rare and exceptional local ingredients. The restaurant's name is inspired by "*sooksoo*," a title once given to royal court chefs in the *Joseon* Dynasty. At the heart of Chef Kwon's creativity lies a deep respect for the authentic identity of Korean food. This dedication shines through its fermented flavors—such as sauces aged for five years—and the unique "Kimchi Cart" course featuring eight varieties of kimchi found nowhere else. Highlights include *deodeok sobaki* (stuffed *kimchi*),

pheasant kimchi, hairtail kimchi, yuzu-white kimchi, and even rare layered-kimchi with octopus, abalone, and prawns rolled inside white kimchi. These kimchi varieties, based on recipes from his mother and reinterpreted from ancient books, unfold the true fantasy of Korean cuisine. This authentic experience is the primary reason foreign customers are drawn to Kwonsooksoo.

The restaurant's tables are set lower than usual to accommodate *soban*, individual dining trays traditionally used in Korea. The *juansang* (welcome drink with small appetizers) course—a table laden with dishes such as braised beef trotters, beef jerky, ginkgo nut porridge, *samgyejeon* (chicken soup pancake), roasted sweet potato, sliced raw swordtip squid, and *ssambap* (rice wrapped in vegetables)—is paired with potato liquor and brims with the joy of hospitality. The Korean raw beef tartare, generously sprinkled with finely shredded chanterelle mushrooms and garnished with chestnut, blooms like a luscious flower on the white porcelain plate from Kwangjuyo, preserving its nutty flavor and tender texture. Could this be the diverse expression of Chef Kwon, who excels at elevating natural flavors to their highest potential? The turnip and perilla oil dish, topped with coriander leaves and smoked caviar on roasted turnip, creates a refreshing combination through the crispness of the turnip and the subtle saltiness of caviar. Gazing at the *Ilwolobongdo* painting, on the wall, depicting the sun, moon, and five peaks, you experience a serene moment surrounded by refined elegance and time-honored flavors—the true brilliance of Korean cuisine.

KWONSOOKSOO  
권숙수

4F, 37, Apgujeong-ro 80-gil, Gangnam-gu, Seoul  
@kwonsooksoo

# SOSEOUL HANNAM

The defining impression of **SOSEOUL hannam**, a Michelin-starred Korean fine dining restaurant in Hannam-dong, is its dramatic lyricism—a phrase that captures not only the refined food and space, but also the soundscape and the lingering emotion that follows the immersive, three-hour sensory journey. The name "Soseoul" itself plays on multiple layers: in Korean, it echoes the word for "novel," while in Chinese characters, "素設" suggests simplicity and purity. In English, it carries a trendy nuance, resonating as "So Seoul." Since 2018, Chef Eom Taecheol has focused on meticulous dining experiences that weave taste, presentation, and Korean cultural depth. He reinterprets traditional ingredients with innovation—for instance, transforming rice, the core of Korean cuisine, into crispy *bugak* or soft *tteok* for new textures, or pairing freshly cooked *naengi* (shepherd's purse) pot rice with caviar to create an unexpectedly elevated depth of flavor.

Seated once again at a window-side table for a while, three *ssamchu* (lettuce wraps) dumplings filled with spring cabbage and white kimchi float delicately in a clear broth within a concave bowl by ceramist Kim Namhee, radiating a subtle glow. Braised eel *gangjeong* (crispy glazed dish) with shredded ginger, white kelp, and young garlic leaves, alongside *neobiani* (charcoal-grilled marinated *Hanwoo*) seasoned with pear and soy sauce and paired with deep-fried *haebangpung* (coastal

hog fennel), carefully balances between Korean authenticity and flavors with those beyond.

SOSEOUL hannam's tablescape is a quiet reconstruction of Korean cuisine, built upon somewhat humility. Completing Chef Eom's course feels akin to walking away from a striking painting—its afterimage still vivid in the mind. What makes dining at SOSEOUL hannam such a compelling experience is not only from the food but also from the incorporated artworks, the subtle interplay of light and shadow, and the artisanal details of the furniture. Metal artist Kim Hyunsung's willow leaf sculptures in brass with a tin finish cascade from the ceiling, while ceramist Noh Gippum's ceramic objects gently grace the lower part of the pristine white wall partitions. A single, modest flower adorns the metal handle of a sliding door, and an unexpected brightness for a basement level softly ripples through the *hanji* papered windows. This is why guests linger long after the course concludes with sweet ginger *yakgwa*, candied pine nuts, *taraegwa* (twisted honey cookie), and sweet bean paste cookies.

SOSEOUL HANNAM  
소설 한남

B1F, 21-18, Hannam-daero 20-gil,
Yongsan-gu, Seoul
@soseoul_hannam

# GIWAKANG

**GiwaKang**, an innovative Korean cuisine destination, stands out from its very name. It signifies the warm and powerful energy that flows gently through all living things, quietly settling in each individual's heart. If the finest gift that cuisine can offer is this very transmission of energy, then GiwaKang's tasting course lives up to more than the expectation. Guests are to enter through a passage flanked by an open kitchen on one side and a carefully curated wine cellar on the other, gradually stepping into a dimly lit dining hall. Seated beneath jade-colored curtains and elegant lighting, diners are invited to pause and take in the atmosphere. The meal begins with a whimsical amuse-bouche: a celadon turtle bearing an olive stuffed with pistachio. Throughout the experience, GiwaKang showcases the graceful beauty of Korean aesthetics by presenting celadon pieces with natural curves and subtle jade hues as wine glasses, water cups, and plates. Chef Kang Minchul, trained in classic French culinary

techniques, crafts a contemporary Korean menu that harmonizes European refinement with the richness of traditional Korean flavors. One standout is the soy-marinated raw crab—aged in *Jinjang*, master artisan Ki Soondo's fully matured soy sauce, enhanced by the earthy aroma of truffle. Another feature is the succulence of duck and the deep flavor of eel, perfectly balanced by a house-fermented jujube *gochujang*. These dishes are accompanied by perilla leaves, endive, and chicory, arranged on the plate like a beautifully composed landscape. The taste of GiwaKang—where familiarity and unfamiliarity coexist yet ultimately conclude with comfort—reaches its pinnacle in emotionally resonant desserts. The "Pine Tree," for instance, where mugwort cream, ganache, and ice cream meet crispy textures to emerge with a verdant burst of bittersweet delight.

Time spent at GiwaKang transcends a simple course, it is akin to a profound conversation about what is uniquely Korean. That is because it combines the grammatical structure of gastronomy rooted in tradition—the noble celadon works of ceramist Baek Rahee, sommelier Lee Jungin's delicate wine pairings, and the deep flavors of master Ki Soondo's fermented sauces—a harmony of all five senses. On one wall of the kitchen, a wooden plaque reads "Love and Sincerity." It quietly reflects the heartfelt intention behind every dish, offering guests not only a special dinner but a deeply genuine experience.

GIWAKANG  
기와강

4F, 9, Nonhyeon-ro 152-gil, Gangnam-gu, Seoul  
@giwakang

# LA YEON

Located on the twenty-third floor of The Shilla Seoul, one of the city's premier five-star hotels, **La Yeon** offers a refined sense of hospitality from the moment you step inside the building to the moment you arrive at the restaurant. Centered on the concept of "the finest Korean cuisine served with grace and dignity," La Yeon is a fine-dining restaurant that exquisitely blends tradition with a modern interpretation of Korean culinary arts. Since its opening in 2013, La Yeon has remained committed to delivering consistent, impeccable flavors through the use of carefully selected seasonal ingredients. Its culinary excellence has been recognized not only by the *Michelin Guide* but also by *LA LISTE.*, where La Yeon became the first Korean restaurant to earn top rankings. Executive Chef Kim Sungil, who celebrates 37 years with The Shilla this year, brings a deep understanding of traditional Korean cuisine. Alongside him, Chef Cha Doyoung, with 20 years of experience, adds a touch of

contemporary creativity. Their combined expertise creates a harmonious synergy that defines La Yeon's distinctive culinary identity.

As you become mesmerized by the serene view of Namsan Mountain outside the window, the table is set with a chilled red seabream with white kimchi sauce inspired by the landscape itself—an elegant introduction to the course. La Yeon's course prominently features rare dishes inspired by ancient Korean cookbooks, further heightening anticipation. The harmony of *suran* (poached eggs), a royal court dish recorded in the *Joseon*-era cookbooks "*Jubangmun*" and "*Siuijeonseo*," and delicately presented fermented steamed buns in a bamboo basket, so to speak, offers a rich yet clean taste. Served in a concave *bangjja yugi* (Korean traditional bronzeware) bowl handcrafted by artisan Lee Bongju, is none other than *galbijjim* (warm braised short rib). This premium *Hanwoo* dish with its

subtle sweetness and the tenderly resilient texture of the meat, is a signature dish whose flavor is unforgettable to anyone who experiences La Yeon. The *sotbap* (rice cooked in a stone pot), prepared with three specially selected indigenous rice varieties—*Mettwaejichalbyeo*, *Gwido*, and *Jagwangdo*—offers a perfectly chewy texture that, combined with fragrant sesame oil, provides a satisfying finish. La Yeon's dedication to acutely exploring the tradition and present of Korean cuisine while maximizing the inherent flavors of the ingredients is evident throughout the dishes. To experience Seoul in its most authentic and elegant form, La Yeon is not to be missed.

LA YEON  
라연

23F, Shilla Hotel, 249, Dongho-ro, Jung-gu, Seoul  
@theshilla_seoul

# BICENA

Located on the eighty-first floor of the Signiel Tower, **BICENA** offers more than just fine dining—it delivers a transcendent moment where heavenly flavors meet dramatic elevation. The name "BICENA," meaning to empty, to fill, and to share, encapsulates the restaurant's philosophy. Operated by Gaon Society, BICENA, the culinary branch of Kwangjuyo Group—a prestigious ceramics company founded in 1963—is a contemporary fine-dining destination where cuisine and craft are inseparable. It is a space where food culture is experienced through both dish and vessel.

Chef Jun Kwangsik expresses the essence of Korean cuisine by infusing the finest ingredients with a sense of Korean beauty, creating dishes that evoke both empathy and heaing. He is well-renowned for his creative takes on Korean classics, such as pairing meat with fresh leafy vegetables for wrapping or light kimchi-style salads, or elevating traditional fermented sauces with caviar. The menu features poetic names like

"*Ilwol* (Sun & Moon)," "*Sancheon* (Mountains & Streams)," "*Juksong* (Bamboo Pine)," and "*Guhak* (Nine Cranes)," inspired by the *Sipjangsaeng*—the ten symbols of longevity in Korean culture. Reinforcing this identity, a glass display at the entrance showcases two historical ceramic masterpieces: a Celadon cup and stand, inlaid with a design of chrysanthemums from the *Goryeo* period, and a white porcelain covered bowl with peony design in underglaze blue from the *Joseon*

dynasty. These rare pieces hint at the deeper cultural narrative BICENA is telling.

One of the welcoming dishes is a wheat wrap filled with carrot, egg, cucumber, mushroom, and beef jerky, all rolled in a black sesame crêpe for a burst of flavors in a single bite. The *yukhoe*, made from *Hanwoo* sirloin aged for thirty days and then dry-aged for another six days, offers a uniquely chewy texture. Spring is captured in the mugwort fritter, where flounder is coated in mugwort batter, fried to a crisp, and topped with yellow rapeseed flower and Chinese artichoke, evoking the freshness of the season. Above all, BICENA's true charm lies in how the subtle

hues and natural textures of Kwangjuyo's diverse ceramics enhance the dining experience, allowing guests to rediscover the beauty of Korean tableware. A matte-finish plate with bold black brushstrokes, a 24-faceted porcelain cup, a dish lined with flowing *yeonlimun* (entwined pattern) techniques—each piece is chosen to enhance the narrative of the food it holds. Dessert continues this grace between elegance and playfulness. A scoop of ice cream infused with five traditional Korean ingredients—ginger, cinnamon dried tangerine peel, jujube, and dried chestnut—delivers a nostalgic yet refreshing finish. A small bite of *gotgamran*, a candied dried persimmon filled with softened nuts, bursts with gentle sweetness, especially when paired with *sujeonggwa*, a cinnamon-ginger tea. It is a tender finale, where flavor and emotion intertwine. The smooth progression of flavors fosters a shared appreciation, perhaps explaining the unusually intimate atmosphere where the kitchen and tables feel closely connected at BICENA.

BICENA
비채나

81F, 300, Olympic-ro, Songpa-gu, Seoul
@bicena_seoul

# TERMS BASED ON
# THE KOREAN CULTURE

# GALLERY

**SEOUL MUSEUM OF CRAFT ART (SeMoCA)**

1  Silla (Silla Dynasty)
   One of the Three Kingdoms of ancient Korea, existing from 57 BCE to 935 CE alongside Goguryeo and Baekje.

2  Goryeo (Goryeo Dynasty)
   A kingdom that unified the Later Three Kingdoms in 918 and ruled the Korean Peninsula for 474 years.

3  Joseon (Joseon Dynasty)
   The kingdom founded by Yi Seonggye after the fall of Goryeo, lasting from 1392 to 1910 under the rule of 27 monarchs.

4  Ottchil
   A traditional Korean lacquer technique that uses tree sap to create a durable, glossy, and protective finish on wooden objects.

5  Soban
   A small wooden table used for serving or eating food.

**ARUMJIGI**

6  Gyeongbokgung
   The main royal palace of the Joseon Dynasty, built in 1395 and located in Sejong-ro, Jongno-gu, Seoul.

7  Hanok
   A traditional Korean house built in the vernacular architectural style.

8  Hanbok
   Korea's traditional attire, passed down since ancient times.

9  Hanji
   Traditional Korean paper made from mulberry bark using unique local techniques.

**GOBOKII**

10 Bandaji
   A type of chest with a front panel that folds down halfway, used for storing clothes, dishes, and other household items.

**MOSOON**

11 Deoksugung Daehanmun
   The main gate of Deoksugung Palace, which served as the imperial palace during the Korean Empire.

12 Nong
   A small chest or cabinet, typically made from willow or broomwood, used to store clothing or household items.

**MONOHA HANNAM**

13 Yeonrimun technique
   A ceramic technique that creates irregular patterns by mixing clays of different properties and colors.

# SHOP

**AREAPLUS**

1  Yutnori (Yut Game)
   A traditional Korean board game enjoyed from New Year's Day to the first full moon of the lunar year. Played with special sticks called Yut, it is a folk game in which anyone can participate and have fun together.

**JANGSAENGHO**

2  Min Byeongok House (Gyeongun-dong Min Byeongok House)
   A modernized hanok designed by renowned architect Park Gilryong in the 1930s during the Japanese colonial period.

3  Hwajodo (Flower-and-Bird Painting)
   A genre of East Asian painting featuring flowers and birds, considered the third major category

after landscape and figure paintings.

4 Sarangbang
A study and reception room for mostly men in traditional Korean houses.

## WOL HANNAM

5 Chaekgado
A genre of still-life paintings centered around scholars' bookshelves, including books, inkstones, ink sticks, and brush holders, popular in Korea during the 18th-19th centuries.

## ILSANGYEOBACK

6 Dalhangari
A large, round porcelain jar made during the late Joseon Dynasty, especially after the 18th century.

## HOHODANG

7 Dano
A traditional holiday on the fifth day of the fifth lunar month, considered a major holiday as it's believed to be the day with the strongest positive energy of the year.

8 Dongji (The winter solstice)
The twenty-second of the 24 seasonal divisions, the day with the longest night and shortest day of the year.

9 Baenaet-jeogori
A newborn baby's first upper garment without a collar or front overlap.

10 Ipchuncheop
New Year's greeting papers attached to doors or house pillars to celebrate and wish for good fortune during Ipchun, the first of the 24 seasonal divisions.

11 Bojagi
A square piece of cloth used for wrapping or covering objects.

12 Yangdan
A relatively thick brocade fabric with patterns woven into a satin weave background, used for hanbok.

13 Nobang
A stiff silk fabric made with silk threads in plain weave.

14 Dongshimgyeol
A traditional Korean knot symbolizing two hearts united as one. It represents harmony, deep connection, and enduring affection between people.

## KYUBANGDOGAM

15 Mumyeong
Traditional Korean cotton fabric woven from spun cotton, widely used for commoners' clothing.

16 Chunpo
A stiff, cool-feeling fabric woven from a blend of silk and ramie threads.

17 Sagunja
An East Asian painting motif depicting plum blossom, orchid, chrysanthemum, and bamboo, each symbolizing noble virtues.

## NARRATIVE OBJECT

18 Kkeomeok smoking firing technique
A technique where ceramics fired above 1,000°C in a kiln are immediately placed in sawdust.

## TABLE OF CRAFT (TOC.)

19 Hansan mosi
High-quality ramie fabric produced in the Hansan region of Seocheon, Chungcheongnam-do, prized as a summer textile.

# TEA HOUSE

## SANSUHWA TEAHOUSE

1 Gongdobae
A tea vessel used to collect brewed

tea to maintain consistent concentration.

2. Sukwoo
A vessel used to cool hot water to the proper temperature for tea.

3. Gaiwan
A lidded tea cup commonly used in China.

## MONGJAE

4. Dasik
A traditional Korean tea snack made by pressing powdered grains, seeds, or nuts into decorative molds. It's often served during special occasions with tea and comes in various colors and patterns.

## CHACHA TEA CLUB BUKCHON LOUNGE

5. Seokkarae (Rafters)
Rib-like wooden beams that support the roof in traditional Korean wooden architecture.

## 1994SEOUL

6. Jeolgi
Jeolgi refers to the 24 seasonal divisions in the traditional East Asian lunar calendar, based on the sun's position throughout the year. Each jeolgi reflects changes in climate, agriculture, and daily life.

7. Sesipungsok (Seasonal Customs)
Traditional agricultural customs and festivals observed throughout the year according to the farming calendar.

8. Chubun (The autumn equinox)
the moment when day and night are roughly equal in length, marking the beginning of fall in the Northern Hemisphere.

9. Najeonchilgi (Mother-of-Pearl Lacquerware)
A decorative lacquer technique that inlays thin layers of shell onto the surface of furniture or objects.

# DINING

## ONJIUM RESTAURANT

1. Banga
An abbreviation for yangban sadaebu, referring to the Confucian aristocracy and noble families of the Joseon Dynasty.

## RESTAURANT JUEUN

2. Dancheong
The art of painting colorful patterns on the wooden structures and walls of traditional Korean buildings for decoration and protection.

SEOUL SEOUL SEOUL
A GUIDE TO SPACES OF CRAFT IN SEOUL

**WRITER**
Park Sunyoung

**PUBLISHING HOUSE**
RAWPRESS

**PUBLISHING DIRECTOR**
Shin Umi

**PLANNING & COORDINATION**
Park Sunyoung, Bae Danbee

**PROJECT MANAGEMENT & EDITING**
Bae Danbee

**TRANSLATION**
Oh Seunghae

**PROOFREADING**
Héloïse Lassonde, i-Spin

**PHOTOGRAPHY**
Yoon Miyeon

**DESIGN**
REMOTE

**PRINTING**
Dodam Printing

ISBN 979-11-90109-23-9

RAWPRESS is a publishing house specializing in lifestyle content. With a focus on food culture, we explore the contemporary ways of living that enrich and diversify our everyday lives. Through magazines, books, and other publications, we share the unique values and deeper meanings behind these cultural experiences.
@rawpress.co @rawpressbooks

Despite careful editing and proofreading, the publisher accepts no responsibility for any errors or omissions that may remain in this guide.

*"SEOUL SEOUL SEOUL"* is published by RAWPRESS,
44, Seongsuil-ro 12-gil, Seongdong-gu, Seoul, Republic of Korea
rawpress@rawpress.co.kr

All rights reserved.
First Edition, Printed in July 2025

Copyright © 2025 Park Sunyoung
Editorial Copyright © 2025 RAWPRESS